Previously published...

- Maths and Calculator skills for Science Students
  http://amzn.to/2xgED3Q
- Maths (The Chemistry bits) for GCSE Science — May 2016
  http://amzn.to/2jJxyWc
- Science revision Guide — April 2017
- Maths Revision Guide — April 2017
- Summer Start for A-Level Chemistry — May 2017
  http://amzn.to/2suR1e5
- Atoms, Electrons, Structure and Bonding Workbook — June 2017
  http://amzn.to/2tn8Rji
- GCSE Maths Grade 7, 8 and 9 Revision Questions — September 2017
  http://amzn.to/2fGQrrz

Coming soon...

- Complete Maths workbook — due Christmas 2017
- Organic Chemistry Workbook
- Maths for A-Level Chemistry
- Maths (The Physics bits) for GCSE Combined Science
- Maths (The Physics bits) for GCSE Triple Science
- Summer Start for A-Level Physics

Chances are if you want a maths/science book I've written it or I am writing it.

For full book listings visit www.PrimroseKitten.com and follow @primrose_kitten

First published 2017   Copyright; Primrose Kitten ©

Image credits, Images by Lemberg Vector studio, by Macrovector, used under license from Shutterstock.com. Pixabay. https://www.teacherspayteachers.com/Store/The-Cher-Room

Acknowledgements
Thank you to my husband for putting up with my spending every night writing this and for correcting all of my SPG mistakes. To my sons for being the inspiration behind Primrose Kitten.

Hello Lovely Kittens

Thank you so much for purchasing this revision booklet. Many items covered in here is also covered in a corresponding set of videos which I have made neat and accessible on my terrific partner platform: TuitionKit.

On TuitionKit you'll be able to schedule many of my revision videos and partner content to help you organise your revision better, breaking it down into easy to handle bitesize chunks. You'll also find many of my other playlists and great resources from other Science and Maths teachers, as well as super English teachers too.

My videos are free when you sign up at www.tuitionkit.com/primrosekitten Using the discount code "kitten" will also give you a 20% discount on all the other material on the site for all your core GCSE subject revision.

To get a flavour for how TuitionKit's great features will help you revise, go to www.tuitionkit.com and sign up for your free 48-hour trial.

Wishing you all the best with your revision!

Primrose Kitten

xoxo

Table of Content

Revision Techniques 7

Revision Timetable 8

   Planning Tips 8

   Weekday 9

   Weekend 10

Exam command words 11

   Glossary of exam command words 12

   How to answer 6 mark questions 13

Exam dates 14

Maths Skills for Science Students 15

Biology 17

   5 most common mistakes in a biology exam 17

   Topic Guide 18

   Required practical's 18

   Key Words 19

   1 - Cell structure 23

      Knowledge Checklist 23

      Quick fire questions; 25

   2 – Organisation 27

      Knowledge Checklist 27

      Quick fire questions; 30

   3 - Infection and response 33

      Knowledge Checklist 33

      Quick Fire Questions 36

   4 – Bioenergetics 38

      Knowledge Checklist 38

      Quick Fire Questions 40

   5 – Homeostasis and Response 41

      Knowledge Checklist 41

      Quick Fire Questions 46

6 – Inheritance, variation and evolution 49
    Knowledge Checklist 49
    Quick Fire Questions 55

7 – Ecology 57
    Knowledge Checklist 57
    Quick fire Questions 62

Crosswords 64

Chemistry 74

5 most common mistakes in a chemistry exam 74

Important tips 74

Topic Guide 75

Equation Sheet 76

Formula of common acids and compounds 76

Reference table of common formulae 77

The Reactivity Series 78

Required practical's 79

Key Words 80

1 – Atomic Structure and the Periodic Table 82
    Knowledge Checklist 82
    Quick fire questions; 86

2 – Bonding, Structure and the Properties of Matter 89
    Knowledge Checklist 89
    Quick fire questions; 92

3 – Quantitative Chemistry 95
    Knowledge Checklist 95
    Quick fire questions; 98

4 – Chemical Changes 100
    Knowledge Checklist 100
    Quick fire questions; 103

5 – Energy Changes 104
    Knowledge Checklist 104

Quick fire questions;	106
6 – The Rate and Extent of Chemical Change	107
Knowledge Checklist	107
Quick fire questions	110
7 – Organic Chemistry	111
Knowledge Checklist	111
Quick Fire Questions	116
8 – Chemical Analysis	118
Knowledge Checklist	118
Quick Fire Questions	120
9 – Chemistry of the Atmosphere	121
Knowledge Checklist	121
Quick Fire Questions	123
10 – Using Resources	124
Knowledge Checklist	124
Quick Fire Question	127
Crosswords	128
Physics	135
5 most common mistakes in a physics exam	135
Topic Guide	135
Required practical's	136
AQA GCSE Physics Equation Sheet	137
Topic 1 – Energy	137
Topic 2 – Electricity	138
Topic 3 – Particle Model of Matter	138
Topic 5 – Forces	139
Topic 6 – Waves	140
Topic 7 – Magnetism and Electromagnetism	141
1 – Energy	142
Knowledge Checklist	142
Quick fire questions;	145

2 – Electricity 147
Knowledge Checklist 147
Quick fire questions; 151

3 – Particle Model of Matter 153
Knowledge Checklist 153
Quick fire questions; 155

4 – Atomic Structure 156
Knowledge Checklist 156
Quick fire questions; 159

5 – Forces 160
Knowledge Checklist 160
Quick Fire Questions 166

6 – Waves 169
Knowledge Checklist 169
Quick Fire Questions 174

7 – Magnetism and Electromagnets 176
Knowledge Checklist 176
Quick Fire Questions 179

8 – Space Physics – Physics only 180
Knowledge Checklist 180
Quick Fire Questions 181

Crosswords 182

Answers 184

Revision Techniques

https://www.youtube.com/playlist?list=PL7O6CcKg0HaEAmHG0SbleDHfdJOQvUcnM

- Why do you need to revise effectively? Revision techniques #1
- When should I start revising? Revision Techniques #2
- How to find your motivation and stay motivated. Revision Techniques #3
- 5 easy and effective ways to revise and study. Revision Techniques #4
- Flashcards. Revision Techniques #5
- Using past exam papers to study. Revision Techniques #6
- Colour - The easiest way to make study interesting. Revision Techniques #7
- How to revise for the new specification maths exams. Revision Techniques #8
- How to fill MASSIVE gaps in your knowledge. Revision Techniques #9
- How to best use your revision guide. Revision Techniques #10
- How best to use your revision guide, part 2. Revision techniques #11
- The easiest way to improve your grades, which you're going to hate!! Revision Techniques #12
- Study timetable. Revision techniques #13
- Study Timetable - Plan with Me. Revision Techniques #13
- Another easy way to improve your grades, which you're going to hate!! Revision Techniques #14
- Study Space. Revision Techniques #15

Don't believe me? – here are some more links to help you.

The science of revision: nine ways pupils can revise for exams more effectively.

The Guardian. Bradley Busch Psychologist @Inner_drive Tuesday 19 April 2016

Ditch the highlighter and teach a friend. Psychology shows us a lot about how to improve our memory and avoid distractions – here are some dos and don'ts

https://www.theguardian.com/teacher-network/2016/apr/19/students-revise-exams-revision-science?CMP=share_btn_tw

Revision Timetable

Planning Tips

1. Write your timetable in pencil (or make a version on the computer) so you can change things around if necessary.
2. Start by thinking about what activities you can't miss (dinner, clubs or TV programs) and put these into your timetable.
3. Plan in when you need to do your homework to get it in on time
4. On top of your homework time, aim for a minimum of 2 extra hours on a weekday and 4 hours each day over the weekend.
5. Plan to revise for 1 hour per subject each week (this is in addition to homework) fill in the table below to help you work out how much time you need to spend on revision
6. Fill in the timetable spreading out the subjects (e.g., don't do a whole day of Maths, do a bit each day) put contrasting subjects next to each other, to give your brain a break (e.g. English and Physics)
7. Stick to the timetable, it will help ensure you cover each subject and spread out your revision.

Subject	Group	Priority	Number of hours each week
Maths	Core	High (+2 hours)	
English Language	Core	High (+2 hours)	
English Literature	Core	High (+2 hours)	
	A-level choice	High (+2 hours)	
	A-level choice	High (+2 hours)	
	A-level choice	High (+2 hours)	
	A-level choice	High (+2 hours)	
	Subject I struggle with	Medium (+1 hour)	
	Subject I struggle with	Medium (+1 hour)	
	Subject I struggle with	Medium (+1 hour)	
	Subject I struggle with	Medium (+1 hour)	

Weekday

Time	Monday	Tuesday	Wednesday	Thursday	Friday
4.00 - 4.25					
			5-minute break		
4.30 - 4.55					
			5-minute break		
5.00 - 5.25					
			5-minute break		
5.30 - 5.55					
			5-minute break		
6.00 - 6.25					
			5-minute break		
6.30 - 6.55					
			5-minute break		
7.00 - 7.25					
			5-minute break		
7.30 - 7.55					
			5-minute break		
8.00 - 8.25					
			5-minute break		
8.30 - 9.00					

Primrose Kitten – YouTube Tutorials for Science and Maths.

Weekend

Time	Saturday	Time	Sunday
	5-minute break		
	5-minute break		
	5-minute break		
	5-minute break		
	5-minute break		
	5-minute break		

Exam command words

Command words are words in exam questions that give you clues on what the examiners are looking for.

Depending on the command word, your answer to a question will be very different.

There are four main ones you'll come across; give, describe, explain and evaluate.

Give what is in the picture.

For this answer, you simply need to state using one or two words what is in the picture

A dress

Describe what is in the picture.

For this answer, you need to tell the examiners what it looks like, or recall an event or process

An orange halter neck dress with a pale band around the waist.

Explain what is in the picture.

For this answer, you need to give reasons why something is the way it is

The dress is a summer dress so it has a halter neck, it is from the 1950s and shows the style at the time.

Evaluate what is in the picture.

Here you need to give good points, bad points, your opinion and justify your opinion

- This dress is good because it is made from a light fabric so will be cool in summer
- This dress is bad because the colour is too bright
- Overall, I think this is a good dress...
- ... because it is well suited to the purpose of being a summer dress.

Glossary of exam command words

Calculate/ Determine use maths to work out the answer

Choose circle the answer from the selection

Compare what are the similarities and differences

Complete fill in the gaps - pay attention to any given words, some may be used more than once some not at all

Define what does the word mean?

Describe what it looks like, or recall an event or process

Design/ Plan plan something

Draw draw a scientific diagram, not an arty sketch

Estimate give a sensible guess

Evaluate give good points, bad points your option and justify your opinion

Explain give reasons why something is the way it is

Give/Name a short answer

Identify/Label name a part

Justify give and answer and support it with a reason

Measure you might need to get your ruler out for this one

Plan write a method, don't forget your variables, controls and risk assessment

Plot mark points on a graph using an x

Predict/suggest what do you think is going to happen, you may need to use information from the question and knowledge from class

Show give evidence and come to a conclusion

Sketch a rough drawing, a graph doesn't always need number labels on the axis, but it must be an accurate representation

How to answer 6 mark questions

1. Identify the command word, this tells you what the examiners are looking for. This is generally describe, explain or evaluate.
2. Go back over the question and use different colour high-lighter pens to pick out key bits of information.
3. Plan the structure of your question. Table, paragraphs, diagram.
4. Write your answer
5. Check your answer fully answers the question, make sure is it balanced and cover all the points asked for in the question.
6. Check your spelling, punctuation and grammar.

For over 100 examples of 6 mark questions, with example answers, get my book Science 6 mark answers, from my website or Amazon.

Exam dates

Dates might be changed by AQA

Exam	Units covered	2018 exam dates	2019 exam dates
For separate science and combined science 'Trilogy'			
B1	Topics 1-4	15th May 2018 –pm	Released Feb. 2018
B2	Topics 5-7	11th June 2018 - pm	
C1	Topic 1-5	17th May 2018 – am	
C2	Topics 6-10	13th June 2018 - am	
P1	Topics 1-4	23rd May 2018 - pm	
P2	Topics 5-8	15th June 2018 - am	
For combined science 'Synergy'			
Paper 1: Life and environmental sciences		15th May 2018 – pm	
Paper 2: Life and environmental sciences		23rd May 2018 - pm	
Paper 3: Physical sciences		11th June 2018 - am	
Paper 4: Physical sciences		13th June 2018 - am	

All papers

- Contains multiple choice questions, structured questions, closed short answers questions and open long response questions
- 15% based on required practical's
- Maths requirement vary by subject - 10% of the marks in biology, 20% of the marks in chemistry and 30% of the marks in physics.

Separate Science

- 6 papers (2 biology, 2 chemistry and 2 physics, leading to 3 separate GCSEs)
- Each 1 hour 45 minutes
- Each paper is worth 50% of the GCSE
- 100 marks on each paper

Combined Science – Trilogy

- 6 papers (2 biology, 2 chemistry and 2 physics)
- Each 1 hour 15 minutes
- Each paper is worth 16.7% of the GCSE
- 70 marks on each paper

Combined Science – Synergy

- 4 papers – 2 on life and environmental science and 2 on physical science
- Each 1 hour 45 minutes
- Each paper is worth 25% of the GCSE
- 100 marks on each paper

Maths Skills for Science Students

Maths pops up in every exam; roughly 10% of the marks in biology, 20% of the marks in chemistry and 30% of the marks in physics will be based on maths skills

A workbook containing some of the mathsy skills you'll need is available from my website or from here https://youtu.be/LKPK6fZS1lQ

Specification statement — These are the bits the exam board wants you to know, make sure you can do all of these…	Self-assessment			Bits to help if you don't understand	
	First review 4-7 months before exam	Second review 1-2 months before exam	Final review Week before exam	Primrose Kitten	Other places
I can rearrange equations	☺ 😐 ☹	☺ 😐 ☹	☺ 😐 ☹	https://youtu.be/ mcnBaroQi_Q	TuitionKit http://bit.ly/ 2hJhtPP
I can solve algebraic expressions	☺ 😐 ☹	☺ 😐 ☹	☺ 😐 ☹		TuitionKit http://bit.ly/ 2fGCW7I
I can give numbers to a set number of significant figures	☺ 😐 ☹	☺ 😐 ☹	☺ 😐 ☹	https://youtu.be/ LKPK6fZS1lQ	TuitionKit http://bit.ly/ 2wpK2nY
I can write numbers in standard form	☺ 😐 ☹	☺ 😐 ☹	☺ 😐 ☹	https://youtu.be/ LKPK6fZS1lQ	TuitionKit http://bit.ly/ 2xEQdbK
I can use ratios, fractions and percentage	☺ 😐 ☹	☺ 😐 ☹	☺ 😐 ☹		TuitionKit http://bit.ly/ 2wp2vkl TuitionKit http://bit.ly/ 2fYsJnD
I can calculate a mean and understand what to do with anomalous results	☺ 😐 ☹	☺ 😐 ☹	☺ 😐 ☹	https://youtu.be/ LKPK6fZS1lQ	TuitionKit http://bit.ly/ 2xWkbaB

I can use the symbols <, ≪, ≫, >, ∝, ~	☺ 😐 ☹	☺ 😐 ☹	☺ 😐 ☹		
I can find the y intercept from y=mx+c	☺ 😐 ☹	☺ 😐 ☹	☺✓ 😐 ☹		TuitionKit http://bit.ly/ 2yTCdsj
I can determine the gradient of a graph from the graph or from y=mx+c	☺ 😐 ☹	☺ 😐 ☹	☺✓ 😐 ☹		TuitionKit http://bit.ly/ 2xObyQ4
I can draw a tangent on a graph and determine the gradient	☺ 😐 ☹	☺ 😐 ☹	☺✓ 😐 ☹		
I can measure angles	☺ 😐 ☹	☺ 😐 ☹	☺✓ 😐 ☹		TuitionKit http://bit.ly/ 2yUUNQD
I can calculate the area of a triangle	☺ 😐 ☹	☺ 😐 ☹	☺✓ 😐 ☹		TuitionKit http://bit.ly/ 2ykFZ0L
I can calculate the area of a rectangle	☺ 😐 ☹	☺ 😐 ☹	☺✓ 😐 ☹		
I can calculate surface area of a cuboid	☺ 😐 ☹	☺ 😐 ☹	☺✓ 😐 ☹		TuitionKit http://bit.ly/ 2hHVvwG
I can calculate volume of a cuboid	☺ 😐 ☹	☺ 😐 ☹	☺✓ 😐 ☹		TuitionKit http://bit.ly/ 2xUNMki
I can calculate probability	☺ 😐 ☹	☺ 😐 ☹	☺✓ 😐 ☹		TuitionKit http://bit.ly/ 2hK8wpz
I can draw and interpret frequency plots, and histograms	☺ 😐 ☹	☺ 😐 ☹	☺✓ 😐 ☹		TuitionKit http://bit.ly/ 2g79sAF

Biology

5 most common mistakes in a biology exam

1. Not referring to the graphs - if the exam question asks about a graph, make sure you refer to it in your answer. Most marks can be picked up by clearly talking about the graph
2. Ignoring the patterns and relationships – if there is a link between two things then tell the examiner about it, this is probably what they are looking for
3. Describe or explain – getting these two words confused is a common mistake in all exams but it happens more in biology than any other subject. Make sure you know what the difference is
4. Skipping levels – don't just focus on what is at the top and the bottom, remember all those important bits in-between
5. Forgetting the practical work – loads of marks can be picked up by talking about the practical's you have done in class. Just clearly state all the details and risks

Topic Guide

Topic	First review	Second review	Third review
1 – Cell biology			
2 – Organisation			
3 – Infection and response			
4 – Bioenergetics			
5 – Homeostasis and response			
6 – Inheritance, variation and evolution			
7 – Ecology			

Topic	Quick fire questions	Whole topic summary
1 – Cell biology	https://youtu.be/E9ZiTAaRC-E	
2 – Organisation	https://youtu.be/QnsRz0Xhup8	
3 – Infection and response	https://youtu.be/pq3B_sozPCo	
4 – Bioenergetics	https://youtu.be/1nuYpKaQ3jA	
5 – Homeostasis and response	https://youtu.be/EMf0FbJI9BU	
6 – Inheritance, variation and evolution	https://youtu.be/IL-dUnKmksY	
7 – Ecology	https://youtu.be/NorHSgd7Yyc	

Required practical's

1. Microscopy
2. Microbiology (Biology only)
3. Osmosis
4. Enzymes
5. Food Tests
6. Photosynthesis
7. Reaction Time
8. Plant Responses
9. Field Investigations
10. Decay (Biology only)

Coming soon!!

Key Words

These are easy marks but only if you know them!

Abiotic	Non-living factors that affect organism
Active transport	Movement of ions or gasses from against the concentration gradient
Adaptation	Change in a species to suit the environment
Adrenal gland	Large gland near the kidneys that releases hormone
Aerobic	Respiration with oxygen
Allele	Different version of gene
Amino acids	Building block of proteins
Amylase	Enzyme that breaks carbohydrates into sugars
Anaerobic	Respiration without oxygen
Antibiotics	Drugs that kill bacteria
Aorta	Major blood vessel that carries oxygenated blood away from the heart
Artery	Thick wall blood vessel that carries oxygenated blood around the body
Asexual reproduction	Reproduction with only one parent, resulting in identical offspring
Aspirin	Painkiller developed from willow bark
Bacteria	Tiny organism that causes illness by releasing toxins
Benign tumour	Lump of cells that are not invading the body
Bile	Produced by the liver, neutralizes stomach acid and emulsifies fats
Biodiversity	The range of different organism that live in an environment
Biotic	Living factors that an organism
Bronchi	Braches of the trachea
Cancer	Uncontrolled cell division within the body
Capillary	Thinned walled blood vessels that allow diffusion of gases and nutrients
Carbon cycle	The movement of carbon through the environment
Carbon dioxide	Gas that has one atom of carbon and two atoms of oxygen
Cardiovascular disease	Narrowing of the blood vessels that can lead to dearth
Carnivore	Only eat animals
Cell	Small structural unit that contains a nucleus and cytoplasm
Cell membrane	Partially permeable membrane that surround the cell and control what goes in and out
Cell wall	Surrounds a cell and help maintain cell shape
Chlorophyll	Green part of a plant
Chloroplast	Where photosynthesis takes place
Chromosome	Long stretch of DNA
Community	The organism that live in a particular environment
Contraception	Mechanism to prevent pregnancy
Cystic fibrosis	Inherited disorder that cause damage to lungs

Cytoplasm	Jelly like substance within a cell
Deoxyribose nucleic acid	Long strand of bases that contain genes
Diabetes	Inability of the bod to control blood glucose levels
Diffusion	Movement of ions or gasses from a high concentration to a low concentration
Digestive system	Organ system that absorbs nutrients from food
Digitalis	Heart drug that comes from foxglove plants
Diploid	Two copies of each chromosome
Dominant	Only one copy of the gene is needed to be expressed
Ecology	The study of organism within and environment
Ecosystem	The organism and the habitat they live in
Egg	Female sex cell
Endocrine system	System that controls hormones and responses
Enzyme	Biological catalyst
Evolution	Gradual change in a species over time
Extinction	No breading pair of a species exist
Extremophile	Organism that has adapted to live at extreme conditions
Fatty acids	Can be combined with glycerol to make lipids
Follicle stimulating hormone	Hormone that causes an egg to develop
Fossils	Hard parts of long dead organism
Fungi	Group that includes mushrooms and moulds, they live of decomposing material
Gametes	Sex cells
Gene	Section of DNA, that controls a characteristic
Genome	All of the genes in an organism
Genotype	What genes are present
Glycerol	Can be combined with fatty acid to make lipids
Gonorrhoea	Bacteria that cause a sexual transmitted disease causing smelly discharge from the penis or vagina
Haploid	One copy of each chromosome
Health	State of mental and physical wellbeing
Herbivore	Only eats plant
Heterozygous	Different copies of gene
HIV	Virus that interfere with your body's ability to fight disease
Homoeostasis	Maintaining of a constant internal environment
Homozygous	Identical copies of gene
Hormones	Chemical that causes cells or tissue to respond
Immune system	Organs in the body that work together to defend against disease
In vitro fertilization	Medical treatment to aid getting pregnant
Lipase	Enzyme that breaks fats into fatty acids and glycerol
Lipids	Stores of energy that can be broken down to form fatty acids and glycerol

Luteinizing hormone	Hormone that causes and egg to be released
Malaria	Parasite transmitted by mosquitoes
Malignant tumour	Lump of cells that have developed that ability to travel to other part of the body
Measles	Viral infection causing fever and rash, most common in children
Meiosis	Type of cell division that ends in four different haploid daughter cells
Menstrual cycle	Monthly build up and breakdown of blood in the uterus
Meristem	Plant tissue found at growing tips
Metabolism	Chemical process that occur to maintain life
Mitochondria	Where respiration takes place
Mitosis	Type of cell division that ends in two identical daughter cells
Nucleus	Control centre of the cell, that holds the DNA
Oestrogen	Hormone that acts of the pituitary gland
Omnivore	Eat plants and animals
Organ system	A number of different organs working together towards one function
Osmosis	Transport of water across a partially permeable membrane
Ovaries	In women, these store the eggs
Ovulation	Releases of an egg from the ovaries
Oxygen debt	Arises after anaerobic respiration, needs oxygen to repay
Palisade mesophyll	Upper layer of cell in a leaf
Pancreas	Large gland behind the stomach which produces digestive enzymes
Pathogen	Causes illness
Penicillin	Antibiotic that comes from mould
Phenotypes	What characteristic are present
Phloem	Carries ions around a plant
Photosynthesis	Process that turns carbon dioxide and water into sugars
Pituitary gland	Located at the base of the brain, produces a large number of hormones
Plasma	Fluid part of the blood
Platelets	Small fragments of blood cells that help clotting
Pollution	Harmful substance in an environment
Polydactyly	An extra finger or toe
Predator	Eats prey
Prey	Something that gets eaten
Primary consumer	Herbivore
Protease	Enzyme that breaks proteins into amino acids
Proteins	Long chains of amino acids, that carry out the majority of functions within the body
Protist	Tiny single celled organism that can cause illness
Pulmonary artery	Blood vessel that carries deoxygenated blood from the heart to the lungs
Pulmonary vein	Blood vessel that carries oxygenated blood from the lungs to the heart
Recessive	Two identical copies of the gene are needed to be expressed

Red blood cell	Carries oxygen around the body, has no nucleus
Reflex arc	Nerve pathway including a sensory nerve a synapse and a motor nerve
Respiration	The process of turning sugars into energy, takes place in mitochondria
Respiratory system	Organ system that moves oxygen around the body
Ribosomes	Part of the cell that is responsible for producing proteins
Rose black spot	Fungal disease cause black spot on leave of plants
Salmonella	Bacteria that cause food poisoning
Selective breading	Breading of animals or plants for a particular characteristic
Sexual reproduction	Fusing of male and female gametes
Speciation	New species arising due to environmental change
Sperm	Male sex cell
Spongy mesophyll	Interior layer of cells in a lean
Stem cell	a type of cell that can differentiate into any other type of cell
Testis	In men, these are responsible for the production of sperm
Testosterone	Hormone found predominantly in men
Thyroid	Large gland in the neck which releases hormone
TMV	Virus affecting plants causing a mosaic pattern on leaves
Trachea	Long tube taking air down into the lungs
Transpiration	Process where plant absorb and lose water
Vaccines	Medication that contain inactive or dead virus to help develop immunity
Vein	Blood vessels that have values and carries deoxygenated blood back to the heart
Vena cava	Major blood vessel that carries deoxygenated blood back to the heart
Virus	DNA within a protein coat that divides by invading cells, the resulting cell death causes illness in the host
Water cycle	The movement of water through eh environment
White blood cell	Part of the immune system, produces antibodies and fights pathogens
Xylem	Carries water around a plant

1 - Cell structure

Knowledge Checklist

Specification statement These are the bits the exam board wants you to know, make sure you can do all of these...	Self-assessment			Bits to help if you don't understand	
	First review 4-7 months before exam	Second review 1-2 months before exam	Final review Week before exam	Primrose Kitten	Other places
I can describe the structure of a plant cell and explain the function of all the main parts	☺ 😐 ☹	☺ 😐 ☹	☺ 😐 ☹	https://youtu.be/aM3ZfC1K6W8	TuitionKit http://bit.ly/2x6rlqz
I can describe the structure of an animal cell and explain the function of all the main parts	☺ 😐 ☹	☺ 😐 ☹	☺ 😐 ☹	https://youtu.be/FjF_PO7QVGg	
I can describe the structure of a bacterial cell	☺ 😐 ☹	☺ 😐 ☹	☺ 😐 ☹	https://youtu.be/404tQ7kLDg0	
I can describe the size of different cells	☺ 😐 ☹	☺ 😐 ☹	☺ 😐 ☹		
I can describe and explain a range of specialised cells	☺ 😐 ☹	☺ 😐 ☹	☺ 😐 ☹		TuitionKit http://bit.ly/2fpqhpZ
I can explain cell differentiation	☺ 😐 ☹	☺ 😐 ☹	☺ 😐 ☹		TuitionKit http://bit.ly/2x6l1iI
I can describe how microscopy techniques have changed over time	☺ 😐 ☹	☺ 😐 ☹	☺ 😐 ☹		TuitionKit http://bit.ly/2fr7uuF
I can calculate magnification	☺ 😐 ☹	☺ 😐 ☹	☺ 😐 ☹	https://youtu.be/v-KrUP3bu24	
I can describe how bacteria divide **Biology only**	☺ 😐 ☹	☺ 😐 ☹	☺ 😐 ☹		
I can describe how to prepare an uncontained culture of bacteria using aseptic technique **Biology only**	☺ 😐 ☹	☺ 😐 ☹	☺ 😐 ☹		

I can describe the use of bacterial cultures grown on agar plates **Biology only**	☺ 😐 ☹	☺ 😐 ☹	☺ 😐 ☹	RP2; coming soon	TuitionKit http://bit.ly/2x79KyI
I can describe the location and function of chromosomes	☺ 😐 ☹	☺ 😐 ☹	☺ 😐 ☹		TuitionKit http://bit.ly/2w0hS2y
I can describe each stage in mitosis	☺ 😐 ☹	☺ 😐 ☹	☺ 😐 ☹	https://youtu.be/-P0imnbaHG0	TuitionKit http://bit.ly/2wwUclK
I can define the term stem cell	☺ 😐 ☹	☺ 😐 ☹	☺ 😐 ☹		TuitionKit http://bit.ly/2f0EJE8
I can describe the function of stem cells in embryos, in adult cells and in plants	☺ 😐 ☹	☺ 😐 ☹	☺ 😐 ☹		
I can describe stem cell therapy	☺ 😐 ☹	☺ 😐 ☹	☺ 😐 ☹		
I can discuss the advantages and disadvantages that arise relating to the use of stem cells in medical treatment and ecology	☺ 😐 ☹	☺ 😐 ☹	☺ 😐 ☹		
I can define the term diffusion	☺ 😐 ☹	☺ 😐 ☹	☺ 😐 ☹		TuitionKit http://bit.ly/2h9Z5z9 Total Learn http://bit.ly/2wGqSJE
I can recall which substances are moved by diffusion	☺ 😐 ☹	☺ 😐 ☹	☺ 😐 ☹		
I can describe the process of diffusion	☺ 😐 ☹	☺ 😐 ☹	☺ 😐 ☹		
I can explain how different factors affect diffusion	☺ 😐 ☹	☺ 😐 ☹	☺ 😐 ☹		
I can describe the advantage of having a large surface area to volume ratio and give examples	☺ 😐 ☹	☺ 😐 ☹	☺ 😐 ☹		
I can define the term osmosis	☺ 😐 ☹	☺ 😐 ☹	☺ 😐 ☹		
I can describe the process of osmosis	☺ 😐 ☹	☺ 😐 ☹	☺ 😐 ☹		TuitionKit http://bit.ly/2wj2C4Y
I can define the term active transport	☺ 😐 ☹	☺ 😐 ☹	☺ 😐 ☹		TuitionKit http://bit.ly/2wwUs4c
I can describe the process of active transport	☺ 😐 ☹	☺ 😐 ☹	☺ 😐 ☹		
I can give examples of active transport in action	☺ 😐 ☹	☺ 😐 ☹	☺ 😐 ☹		

Quick fire questions;

This worksheet is fully supported by a video tutorial; https://youtu.be/E9ZiTAaRC-E

1. Label a plant cell.

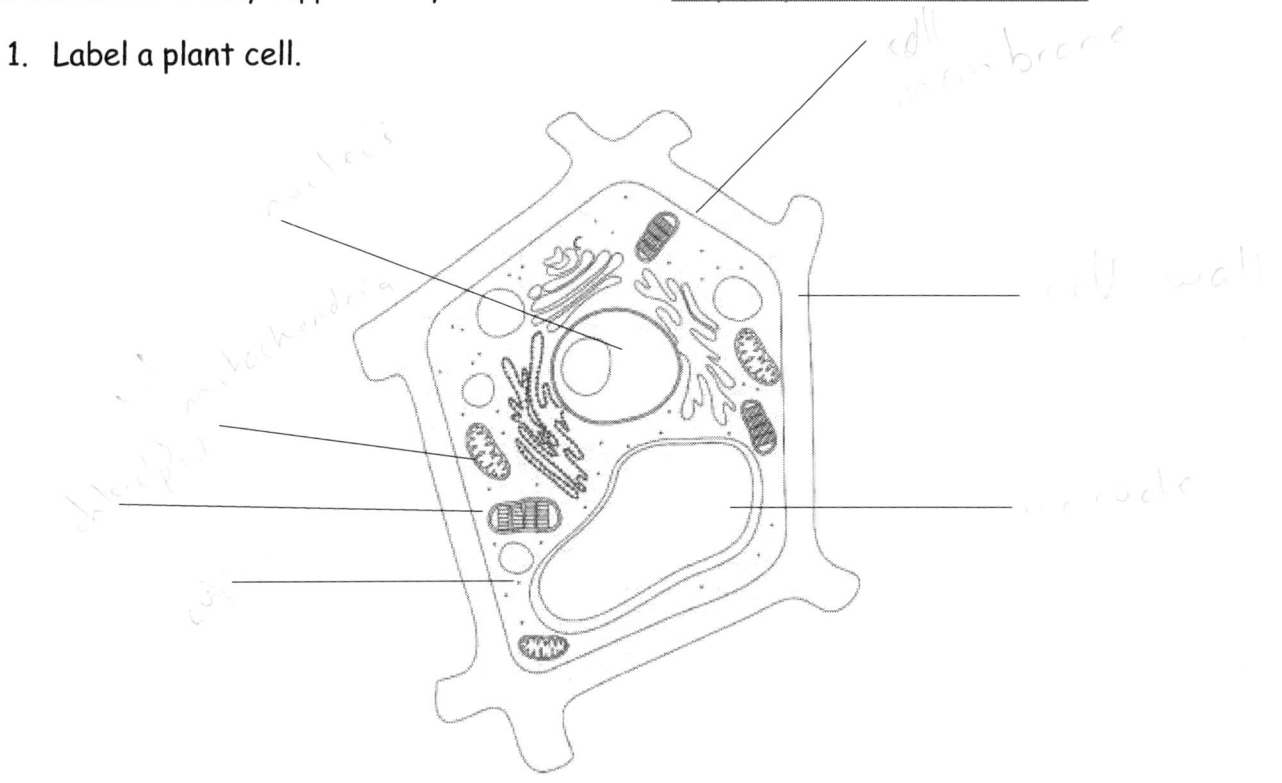

2. Label an animal cell.

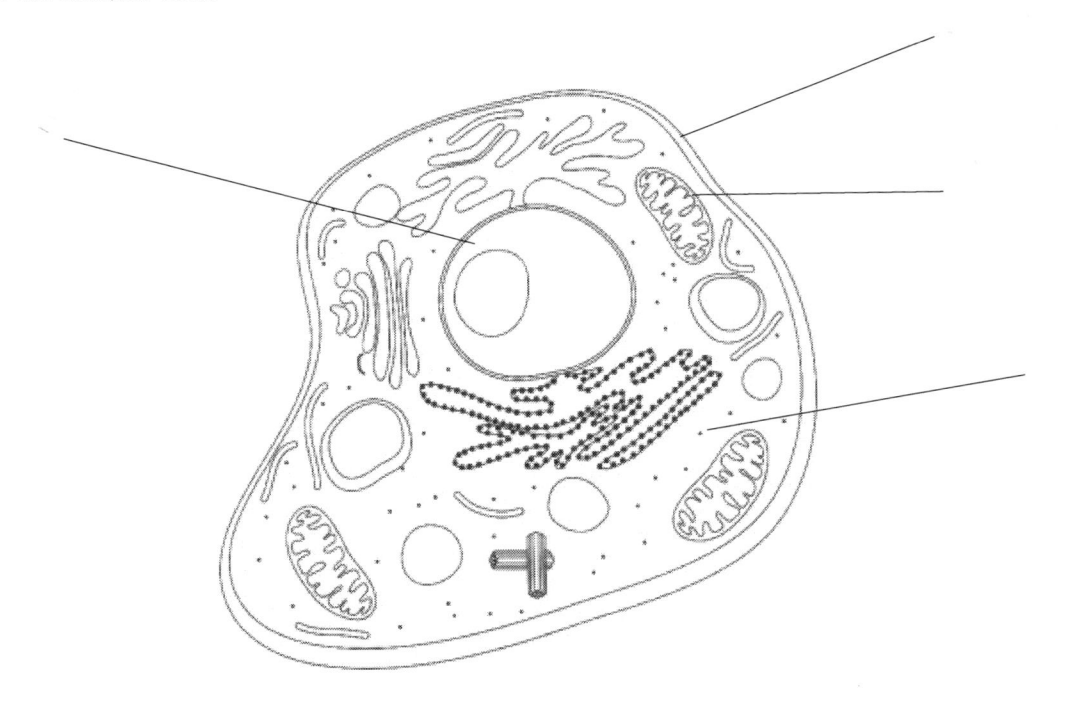

Primrose Kitten – YouTube Tutorials for Science and Maths.   25

3. Label a bacteria cell.

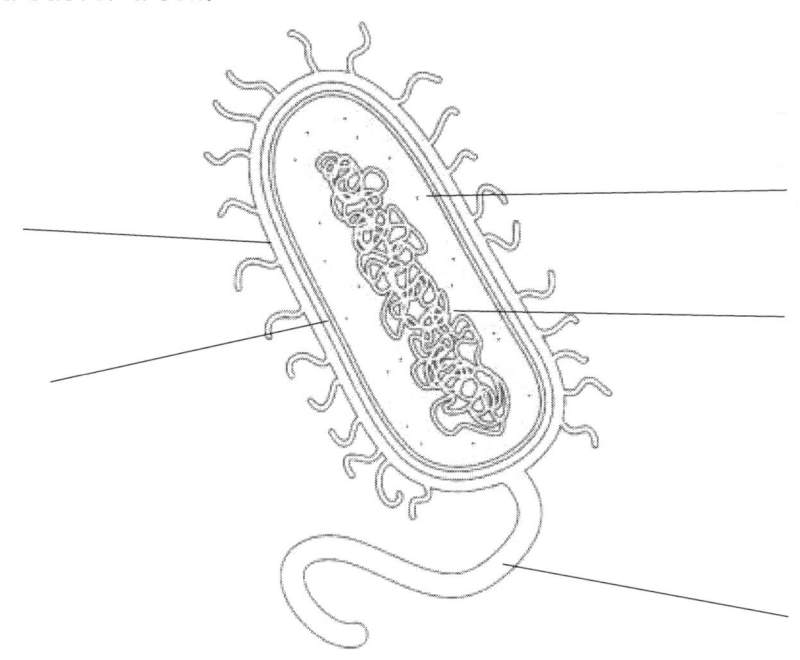

4. Give two different specialist cells.
5. What is differentiation?
6. How do you calculate magnification?
7. Where are chromosomes?
8. What do chromosomes do?
9. What is mitosis?
10. What is a stem cell?
11. What is diffusion?
12. What is osmosis?
13. What is active transport?

2 – Organisation

Knowledge Checklist

Specification statement These are the bits the exam board wants you to know, make sure you can do all of these...	Self-assessment			Bits to help if you don't understand	
	First review 4-7 months before exam	Second review 1-2 months before exam	Final review Week before exam	Primrose Kitten	Other places
I can define the term organ system	☺ 😐 ☹	☺ 😐 ☹	☺ 😐 ☹		TuitionKit http://bit.ly/2h7mcdP
I can describe how the digestive system works	☺ 😐 ☹	☺ 😐 ☹	☺ 😐 ☹		TuitionKit http://bit.ly/2fgFxTF
I can describe how an enzyme works	☺ 😐 ☹	☺ 😐 ☹	☺ 😐 ☹		
I can explain how an enzyme is affected at different temperature and pH	☺ 😐 ☹	☺ 😐 ☹	☺ 😐 ☹		
I can describe the 'lock and key' mechanism	☺ 😐 ☹	☺ 😐 ☹	☺ 😐 ☹		
I can recall for named type of enzyme (amylase, lipase and protease) the location of production and the action	☺ 😐 ☹	☺ 😐 ☹	☺ 😐 ☹		
I can describe the function of enzymes in relation to the digestive system	☺ 😐 ☹	☺ 😐 ☹	☺ 😐 ☹		
I can recall the site of production and uses of bile	☺ 😐 ☹	☺ 😐 ☹	☺ 😐 ☹		
I can recall the organs that make up the respiratory system	☺ 😐 ☹	☺ 😐 ☹	☺ 😐 ☹		
I can describe the structure and function of the heart	☺ 😐 ☹	☺ 😐 ☹	☺ 😐 ☹	https://youtu.be/09WhIK0ueh8	TuitionKit http://bit.ly/2ha0k1h
I can describe the structure and function of the lungs	☺ 😐 ☹	☺ 😐 ☹	☺ 😐 ☹		TuitionKit http://bit.ly/2f1zOmG

I can describe the structure and function of the different types of blood vessel. Aorta, vena cava, pulmonary artery, pulmonary vein, coronary arteries and capillaries.	☺ 😐 ☹	☺ 😐 ☹	☺ 😐 ☹	https://youtu.be/fjrKlYKtfP4	TuitionKit http://bit.ly/2xao8rC
I can define the natural resting heart rate	☺ 😐 ☹	☺ 😐 ☹	☺ 😐 ☹		
I can explain the need for artificial pacemakers	☺ 😐 ☹	☺ 😐 ☹	☺ 😐 ☹		
I can describe the parts that make up blood, and the function of each of these parts	☺ 😐 ☹	☺ 😐 ☹	☺ 😐 ☹		TuitionKit http://bit.ly/2y5lktf
I can recognise a diagram of the different blood calls	☺ 😐 ☹	☺ 😐 ☹	☺ 😐 ☹		
I can explain how different blood cells are adapted to suit a particular function	☺ 😐 ☹	☺ 😐 ☹	☺ 😐 ☹		TuitionKit http://bit.ly/2y5lktf
I can describe the impact cardiovascular disease can have on a person life	☺ 😐 ☹	☺ 😐 ☹	☺ 😐 ☹		TuitionKit http://bit.ly/2h9Auam
I can describe the different ways cardiovascular disease can be treated.	☺ 😐 ☹	☺ 😐 ☹	☺ 😐 ☹		
I can describe the causes of cardiovascular disease	☺ 😐 ☹	☺ 😐 ☹	☺ 😐 ☹		
I can define the term health	☺ 😐 ☹	☺ 😐 ☹	☺ 😐 ☹		
I can describe the impact disease can have on health	☺ 😐 ☹	☺ 😐 ☹	☺ 😐 ☹		
I can describe other factors (diet, stress, life) that can affect health	☺ 😐 ☹	☺ 😐 ☹	☺ 😐 ☹		
I can explain how different types of disease may interact and be triggers	☺ 😐 ☹	☺ 😐 ☹	☺ 😐 ☹		
I can interpret graphic data on diseases and disease trends	☺ 😐 ☹	☺ 😐 ☹	☺ 😐 ☹		
I can describe how to sample epidemiological data	☺ 😐 ☹	☺ 😐 ☹	☺ 😐 ☹		
I can discuss the financial cost of diseases	☺ 😐 ☹	☺ 😐 ☹	☺ 😐 ☹		
I can define the term cancer	☺ 😐 ☹	☺ 😐 ☹	☺ 😐 ☹		
I can differentiate between benign and malignant tumours	☺ 😐 ☹	☺ 😐 ☹	☺ 😐 ☹		

I can recall the different types and location of plant tissues. Epidermal tissue, palisade mesophyll, spongy mesophyll, xylem, phloem and meristem	☺ 😐 ☹	☺ 😐 ☹	☺ 😐 ☹		
I can relate the structure of plant cells to their function, including adaptations.	☺ 😐 ☹	☺ 😐 ☹	☺ 😐 ☹		
I can define the term transpiration	☺ 😐 ☹	☺ 😐 ☹	☺ 😐 ☹		
I can describe how to measure transpiration	☺ 😐 ☹	☺ 😐 ☹	☺ 😐 ☹		
I can explain the effect that temperature/humidity/air movement/light has on transpiration	☺ 😐 ☹	☺ 😐 ☹	☺ 😐 ☹		
I can define an organ system within a plant	☺ 😐 ☹	☺ 😐 ☹	☺ 😐 ☹		

Quick fire questions;

This worksheet is fully supported by a video tutorial; ; https://youtu.be/QnsRz0Xhup8

1. What is an organ system?
2. Name the parts of the digestive system?
3. What happens to enzymes at low temperatures?
4. What happens to enzymes at high temperatures?
5. What happens enzymes are there outside their optimal pH?
6. What is the lock and key mechanism?
7. Where is amylase produced?
8. What does amylase do?
9. Where is lipase produced?
10. What does lipase do?
11. Where is protease produced?
12. What does protease do?
13. Where is bile produced?
14. What does bile do?
15. Label the respiratory system

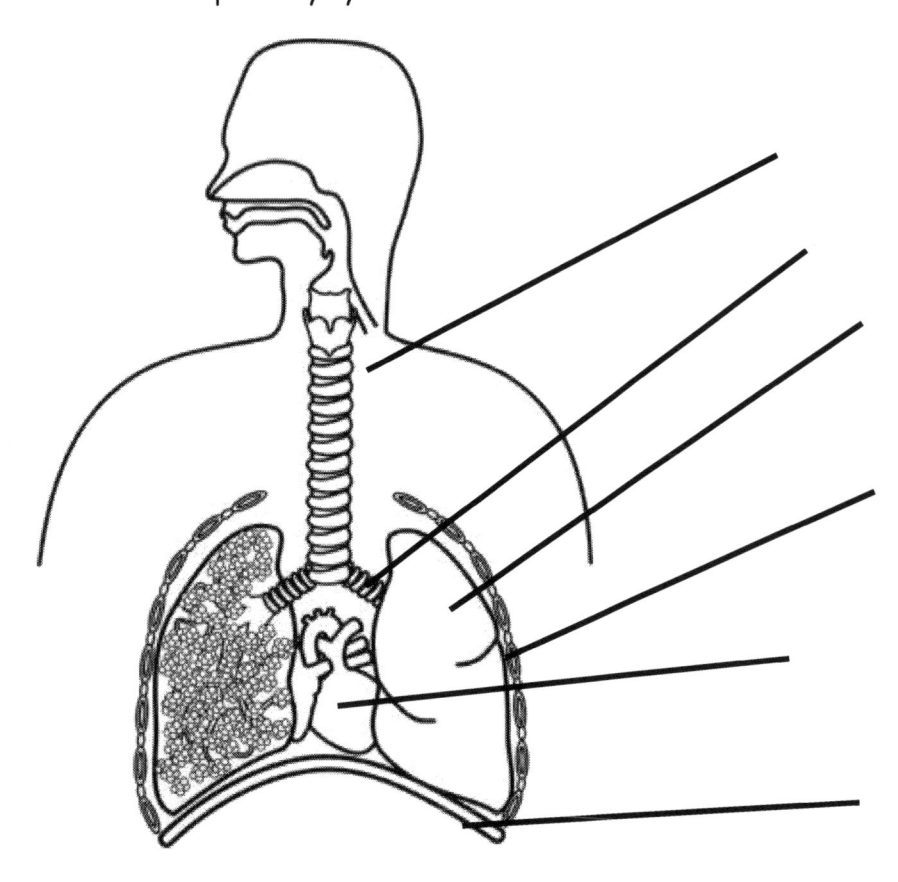

16. What does the heart do?
17. What do the lungs do?
18. Label the heart

19. Draw the path the blood takes through the heart

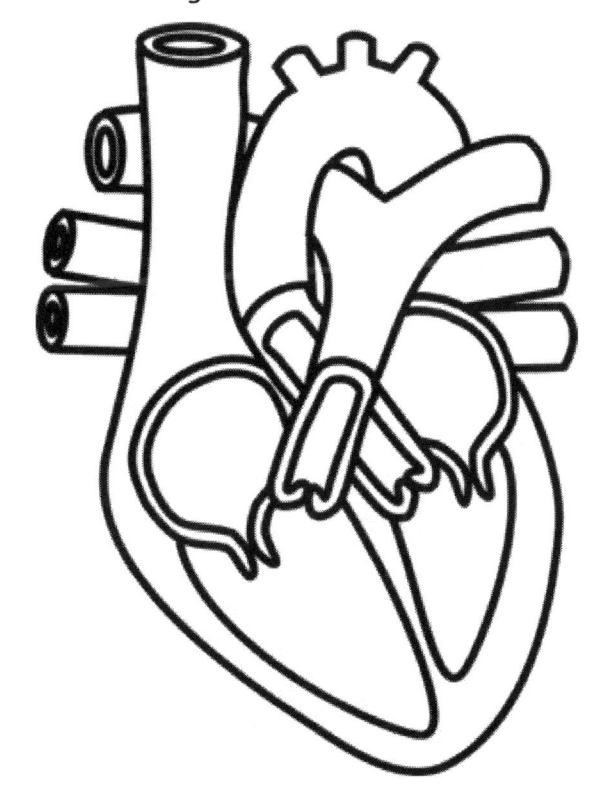

20. What does the aorta do?
21. What does the vena cava do?
22. What does the pulmonary artery do?
23. What does pulmonary vein do?
24. What is natural resting heart rate?
25. Why might you need artificial pacemaker?
26. What do red blood cells do?
27. What do white blood cells do?
28. What do platelets do?
29. What does plasma do?
30. What is cardiovascular disease?
31. What lifestyle factors can affect health?
32. What is cancer?
33. What is a benign tumour?
34. What is a malignant tumour?
35. What is epidermal tissue?
36. What is palisade mesophyll?
37. What is spongy mesophyll?
38. What is the xylem?
39. What is the phloem?
40. What is transpiration?
41. How can we measure transpiration?

3 - Infection and response

Knowledge Checklist

Specification statement These are the bits the exam board wants you to know, make sure you can do all of these...	Self-assessment			Bits to help if you don't understand	
	First review 4-7 months before exam	Second review 1-2 months before exam	Final review Week before exam	Primrose Kitten	Other places
I can describe the range of different ways diseases are caused. Viruses, bacteria, protist or fungi.	☺ 😐 ☹	☺ 😐 ☹	☺ 😐 ☹		TuitionKit http://bit.ly/2f1sjfr http://bit.ly/2h8mD41 http://bit.ly/2fc0uEW
I can describe how diseases are spread in plants and animals	☺ 😐 ☹	☺ 😐 ☹	☺ 😐 ☹		
I can define the term pathogen	☺ 😐 ☹	☺ 😐 ☹	☺ 😐 ☹		
I can describe how bacteria reproduce inside the body	☺ 😐 ☹	☺ 😐 ☹	☺ 😐 ☹		TuitionKit http://bit.ly/2f1sjfr
I can describe how viruses reproduce inside the body	☺ 😐 ☹	☺ 😐 ☹	☺ 😐 ☹		
I can explain how bacteria can make a person feel ill	☺ 😐 ☹	☺ 😐 ☹	☺ 😐 ☹		
I can explain how viruses can make a person feel ill	☺ 😐 ☹	☺ 😐 ☹	☺ 😐 ☹		
I can describe the spread and implication of measles	☺ 😐 ☹	☺ 😐 ☹	☺ 😐 ☹		
I can describe the spread and implication of HIV	☺ 😐 ☹	☺ 😐 ☹	☺ 😐 ☹		
I can describe the spread and implication of TMV	☺ 😐 ☹	☺ 😐 ☹	☺ 😐 ☹		
I can describe the spread and implication of *Salmonella*	☺ 😐 ☹	☺ 😐 ☹	☺ 😐 ☹		TuitionKit

I can describe the spread and implication of gonorrhoea	☺ 😐 ☹	☺ 😐 ☹	☺ 😐 ☹		http://bit.ly/ 2f1sjfr
I can describe the spread and implication of Rose Black Spot	☺ 😐 ☹	☺ 😐 ☹	☺ 😐 ☹		TuitionKit http://bit.ly/ 2h8mD41
I can describe the spread and implication of malaria	☺ 😐 ☹	☺ 😐 ☹	☺ 😐 ☹		TuitionKit http://bit.ly/ 2fc0uEW
I can describe how the body protects itself from disease, including skin, nose, trachea, bronchi and stomach	☺ 😐 ☹	☺ 😐 ☹	☺ 😐 ☹		TuitionKit http://bit.ly/ 2w1fY1u
I can explain the role of the immune system	☺ 😐 ☹	☺ 😐 ☹	☺ 😐 ☹		
I can describe the different roles white blood cells play in the immune system	☺ 😐 ☹	☺ 😐 ☹	☺ 😐 ☹		
I can describe how vaccination can prevent illness	☺ 😐 ☹	☺ 😐 ☹	☺ 😐 ☹		
I can explain how vaccines work	☺ 😐 ☹	☺ 😐 ☹	☺ 😐 ☹		
I can explain the need for antibiotics	☺ 😐 ☹	☺ 😐 ☹	☺ 😐 ☹		
I can explain how antibiotics work	☺ 😐 ☹	☺ 😐 ☹	☺ 😐 ☹		TuitionKit http://bit.ly/ 2fq3uue
I can describe the problem of emerging antibiotic resistance	☺ 😐 ☹	☺ 😐 ☹	☺ 😐 ☹		
I can describe the use of painkillers	☺ 😐 ☹	☺ 😐 ☹	☺ 😐 ☹		
I can describe the process involved in developing a new drug and bringing it to market	☺ 😐 ☹	☺ 😐 ☹	☺ 😐 ☹		TuitionKit http://bit.ly/ 2y5oIV1
I can describe how digitalis, aspirin and penicillin were discovered	☺ 😐 ☹	☺ 😐 ☹	☺ 😐 ☹		
I can recall that new drugs are tested for toxicity, efficacy and dose	☺ 😐 ☹	☺ 😐 ☹	☺ 😐 ☹		
I can describe how monoclonal antibodies are produced **Biology only** **Higher tier only**	☺ 😐 ☹	☺ 😐 ☹	☺ 😐 ☹		TuitionKit http://bit.ly/ 2fq3uue

I can describe how monoclonal antibodies can be used **Biology only** **Higher tier only**	☺ 😐 ☹	☺ 😐 ☹	☺ 😐 ☹		
I can evaluate the advantages and disadvantages of monoclonal antibodies **Biology only** **Higher tier only**	☺ 😐 ☹	☺ 😐 ☹	☺ 😐 ☹		
I can describe how a disease can affect a plant **Biology only** **Higher tier only**	☺ 😐 ☹	☺ 😐 ☹	☺ 😐 ☹		TuitionKit http://bit.ly/2jzh3Me
I can recall how plant disease can be identified **Biology only** **Higher tier only**	☺ 😐 ☹	☺ 😐 ☹	☺ 😐 ☹		
I can describe the range of pathogens that can infect a plant **Biology only**	☺ 😐 ☹	☺ 😐 ☹	☺ 😐 ☹		
I can recall the spread of and damage done by tobacco mosaic virus **Biology only**	☺ 😐 ☹	☺ 😐 ☹	☺ 😐 ☹		
I can recall the spread of and damage done by black spot disease **Biology only**	☺ 😐 ☹	☺ 😐 ☹	☺ 😐 ☹		
I can recall the spread of and damage done by aphids **Biology only**	☺ 😐 ☹	☺ 😐 ☹	☺ 😐 ☹		
I can explain how plants can be damaged by ion deficiency **Biology only**	☺ 😐 ☹	☺ 😐 ☹	☺ 😐 ☹		
I can describe the range of plant defences, including physical, chemical and mechanical **Biology only**	☺ 😐 ☹	☺ 😐 ☹	☺ 😐 ☹		TuitionKit http://bit.ly/2y5kpJp

Quick Fire Questions

This worksheet is fully supported by a video tutorial; https://youtu.be/pq3B_sozPCo

1. Define pathogen.
2. What is a virus?
3. What is bacteria?
4. What is a protist?
5. What is fungi?
6. How can diseases be spread in plants?
7. How can diseases be spread in animals?
8. How do bacteria reproduce inside the body?
9. How do viruses reproduce inside body?
10. How can bacteria make a person feel ill?
11. How can a virus make a person feel ill?
12. What is measles?
13. What is HIV?
14. What is TMV?
15. What is salmonella?
16. What is gonorrhoea?
17. What is Rose Black Spot?
18. What is malaria?
19. How does the skin help protect the body?
20. How does the nose help protect the body?
21. How does the trachea help protect the body?
22. How does the bronchi help protect the body?
23. How does the stomach help protect the body?
24. What is the role of the immune system?
25. What do white blood cells do?
26. How do vaccinations work?
27. What are antibiotics?
28. What is antibiotic resistance?
29. What are painkillers for?
30. Where it is digitalis come from?

31. Where does aspirin come from?

32. Where does penicillin come from?

33. What are the three things that new drugs need to be tested for?

4 – Bioenergetics

Knowledge Checklist

| Specification statement

These are the bits the exam board wants you to know, make sure you can do all of these...	Self-assessment			Bits to help if you don't understand	
	First review 4-7 months before exam	Second review 1-2 months before exam	Final review Week before exam	Primrose Kitten	Other places
I can recall the word and symbol equation for photosynthesis	☺ 😐 ☹	☺ 😐 ☹	☺ 😐 ☹		TuitionKit http://bit.ly/ 2xaLKwl
I can describe the transfer of energy in photosynthesis	☺ 😐 ☹	☺ 😐 ☹	☺ 😐 ☹		
I can explain how different factors affect the rate of photosynthesis. Including temperature, light intensity, carbon dioxide concentration and the amount of chlorophyll	☺ 😐 ☹	☺ 😐 ☹	☺ 😐 ☹		TuitionKit http://bit.ly/ 2jyc7r2
I can explain that more than one factor may be limiting the rate of photosynthesis **Higher tier only**	☺ 😐 ☹	☺ 😐 ☹	☺ 😐 ☹		
I can explain the graphs showing how a limiting factor will affect the rate of photosynthesis **Higher tier only**	☺ 😐 ☹	☺ 😐 ☹	☺ 😐 ☹		
I can describe what the glucose produced in photosynthesis can be used for	☺ 😐 ☹	☺ 😐 ☹	☺ 😐 ☹		TuitionKit http://bit.ly/ 2fcwetD
I can recall the respiration is an exothermic reaction	☺ 😐 ☹	☺ 😐 ☹	☺ 😐 ☹		
I can recall the word and symbol equation for respiration	☺ 😐 ☹	☺ 😐 ☹	☺ 😐 ☹		
I can describe the process of aerobic respiration; in regard to oxygen, the products and the amount of energy	☺ 😐 ☹	☺ 😐 ☹	☺ 😐 ☹		

I can describe the process of anaerobic respiration; in regard to oxygen, the products and the amount of energy	☺ ☻ ☹	☺ ☻ ☹	☺ ☻ ☹		TuitionKit http://bit.ly/2xGYYSV
I can describe what an organism needs energy for	☺ ☻ ☹	☺ ☻ ☹	☺ ☻ ☹		
I can recall the equation for anaerobic respiration	☺ ☻ ☹	☺ ☻ ☹	☺ ☻ ☹		
I can recall the equation for anaerobic respiration in plants and yeast cells	☺ ☻ ☹	☺ ☻ ☹	☺ ☻ ☹		
I can explain the importance of anaerobic respiration in plants and yeast cells for the food industry	☺ ☻ ☹	☺ ☻ ☹	☺ ☻ ☹		
I can recall the need for energy during exercise	☺ ☻ ☹	☺ ☻ ☹	☺ ☻ ☹		TuitionKit http://bit.ly/2wwYhXj http://bit.ly/2fr4CO8
I can describe the effect of exercise on the body	☺ ☻ ☹	☺ ☻ ☹	☺ ☻ ☹		
I can define the term oxygen debt	☺ ☻ ☹	☺ ☻ ☹	☺ ☻ ☹		
I can explain how an oxygen debt can be repaid	☺ ☻ ☹	☺ ☻ ☹	☺ ☻ ☹		

Higher tier only

I can define the term metabolism	☺ ☻ ☹	☺ ☻ ☹	☺ ☻ ☹		TuitionKit http://bit.ly/2h8HcRi
I can explain the role of sugars; amino acids; fatty acids; glycerol; carbohydrates; proteins and lipids	☺ ☻ ☹	☺ ☻ ☹	☺ ☻ ☹		
I can describe the use of energy in the synthesis of new molecules	☺ ☻ ☹	☺ ☻ ☹	☺ ☻ ☹		
I can describe the conversion of glucose to starch, glycogen and cellulose	☺ ☻ ☹	☺ ☻ ☹	☺ ☻ ☹		
I can describe the formation of lipids from glycerol and fatty acids	☺ ☻ ☹	☺ ☻ ☹	☺ ☻ ☹		
I can describe the synthesis of proteins from amino acids	☺ ☻ ☹	☺ ☻ ☹	☺ ☻ ☹		
I can describe the synthesis of amino acids from glucose and nitrate ions	☺ ☻ ☹	☺ ☻ ☹	☺ ☻ ☹		
I can describe the breakdown of proteins, forming urea	☺ ☻ ☹	☺ ☻ ☹	☺ ☻ ☹		

Quick Fire Questions

This worksheet is fully supported by a video tutorial; https://youtu.be/1nuYpKaQ3jA

1. What is the word equation for photosynthesis?
2. What is the chemical symbol for carbon dioxide?
3. What is the chemical symbol for water?
4. What is the chemical symbol for oxygen gas?
5. What is the chemical symbol for glucose?
6. What is the symbol equation for photosynthesis?
7. How is energy transferred in photosynthesis?
8. What factors might affect photosynthesis?
9. How does temperature affect photosynthesis?
10. How does light intensity affect photosynthesis?
11. How does carbon dioxide concentration affect photosynthesis?
12. Sketch the graph to show how light intensity affect photosynthesis (Higher tier only)
13. Sketch the graph to show how temperature affects photosynthesis (Higher tier only)
14. Sketch the graph to show how carbon dioxide concentration affects photosynthesis (Higher tier only)
15. Is respiration exothermic or endothermic?
16. What is the word equation for respiration?
17. What is the symbol equation for respiration?
18. What is anaerobic respiration?
19. What is equation for anaerobic respiration?
20. What is anaerobic respiration in yeast cells?
21. How are the products of anaerobic respiration useful in the food industry?
22. What is oxygen debt?
23. Define metabolism.
24. What do sugars do?
25. What do amino acids do?
26. What do fatty acids do?
27. What does glycerol do?
28. What do carbohydrates do?
29. What do proteins do?
30. What do lipids do?
31. What can glucose be converted to?
32. What are lipids formed from?
33. What are proteins formed from?
34. What are amino acid formed from?
35. What do proteins are broken down into?

5 – Homeostasis and Response

Knowledge Checklist

Specification statement These are the bits the exam board wants you to know, make sure you can do all of these…	Self-assessment			Bits to help if you don't understand	
	First review 4-7 months before exam	Second review 1-2 months before exam	Final review Week before exam	Primrose Kitten	Other places
I can define the term homoeostasis	☺ 😐 ☹	☺ 😐 ☹	☺ 😐 ☹		TuitionKit http://bit.ly/2x43Tg3
I can explain the need for homoeostasis within the context of the human body, including; blood glucose, temperature and water	☺ 😐 ☹	☺ 😐 ☹	☺ 😐 ☹		
I can describe the role of receptors; the brain; the CNS; the pancreas; effectors, muscles; glands in homeostasis	☺ 😐 ☹	☺ 😐 ☹	☺ 😐 ☹		
I can describe the structure of the nervous system	☺ 😐 ☹	☺ 😐 ☹	☺ 😐 ☹		TuitionKit http://bit.ly/2fc8hTp
I can describe how the nervous system works in reacting to surroundings and coordinating behaviour	☺ 😐 ☹	☺ 😐 ☹	☺ 😐 ☹		
I can describe the path a signal takes along the receptor via the CNS	☺ 😐 ☹	☺ 😐 ☹	☺ 😐 ☹		
I can explain a reflex arc	☺ 😐 ☹	☺ 😐 ☹	☺ 😐 ☹		
I can describe the function of the brain **Biology only**	☺ 😐 ☹	☺ 😐 ☹	☺ 😐 ☹		TuitionKit http://bit.ly/2f2c95n
I can identify the different parts of the brain **Biology only**	☺ 😐 ☹	☺ 😐 ☹	☺ 😐 ☹		

I can explain the problems with investigating brain function **Biology only** **Higher tier only**	☺ 😐 ☹	☺ 😐 ☹	☺ 😐 ☹		
I can describe how doctors can map regions of the brain **Biology only** **Higher tier only**	☺ 😐 ☹	☺ 😐 ☹	☺ 😐 ☹		
I can describe the structure of the eye **Biology only**	☺ 😐 ☹	☺ 😐 ☹	☺ 😐 ☹	https://youtu.be/wr3RWxV1JX8	TuitionKit http://bit.ly/2f1zkNn
I can explain the function of the different parts of the eye **Biology only**	☺ 😐 ☹	☺ 😐 ☹	☺ 😐 ☹		
I can describe what happens to the eye when it focuses on near or far objects **Biology only**	☺ 😐 ☹	☺ 😐 ☹	☺ 😐 ☹		
I can describe short sightedness and long sightedness **Biology only**	☺ 😐 ☹	☺ 😐 ☹	☺ 😐 ☹	https://youtu.be/aRDt8PUhv4c	
I can explain how short sightedness and long sightedness can be corrected **Biology only**	☺ 😐 ☹	☺ 😐 ☹	☺ 😐 ☹		
I can interpret ray diagrams **Biology only**	☺ 😐 ☹	☺ 😐 ☹	☺ 😐 ☹		
I can describe how the body controls internal temperature **Biology only**	☺ 😐 ☹	☺ 😐 ☹	☺ 😐 ☹		TuitionKit http://bit.ly/2x4kW1p
I can explain how the body controls internal temperature **Biology only** **Higher tier only**	☺ 😐 ☹	☺ 😐 ☹	☺ 😐 ☹		
I can describe the parts of the endocrine system and how they work together	☺ 😐 ☹	☺ 😐 ☹	☺ 😐 ☹		TuitionKit http://bit.ly/2fbCdis
I can describe the importance of the pituitary gland	☺ 😐 ☹	☺ 😐 ☹	☺ 😐 ☹		
I can identify the locations of the pituitary gland; pancreas; thyroid; adrenal gland; ovary and testes	☺ 😐 ☹	☺ 😐 ☹	☺ 😐 ☹		

I can describe how blood glucose concentration is monitored	☺ 😐 ☹	☺ 😐 ☹	☺ 😐 ☹		TuitionKit http://bit.ly/ 2xH7e5k
I can explain what happens when blood glucose is too high	☺ 😐 ☹	☺ 😐 ☹	☺ 😐 ☹		
I can describe how insulin controls blood glucose levels	☺ 😐 ☹	☺ 😐 ☹	☺ 😐 ☹		
I can describe the cause, symptoms and treatment for type 1 diabetes	☺ 😐 ☹	☺ 😐 ☹	☺ 😐 ☹		
I can describe the cause, symptoms and treatment for type 2 diabetes	☺ 😐 ☹	☺ 😐 ☹	☺ 😐 ☹		
I can explain what happens when blood glucose is too low **Higher tier only**	☺ 😐 ☹	☺ 😐 ☹	☺ 😐 ☹		
I can explain the negative feedback loop that controls blood glucose levels **Higher tier only**	☺ 😐 ☹	☺ 😐 ☹	☺ 😐 ☹		
I can describe the effect osmosis has on cells **Biology only**	☺ 😐 ☹	☺ 😐 ☹	☺ 😐 ☹		
I can describe how water leaves and enters the body **Biology only**	☺ 😐 ☹	☺ 😐 ☹	☺ 😐 ☹		TuitionKit http://bit.ly/ 2h6ZS3T
I can describe what happens to cells if they lose or gain too much water **Biology only**	☺ 😐 ☹	☺ 😐 ☹	☺ 😐 ☹		
I can explain the need for amino acids to be excreted **Biology only** **Higher tier only**	☺ 😐 ☹	☺ 😐 ☹	☺ 😐 ☹		
I can describe the function of the kidneys **Biology only**	☺ 😐 ☹	☺ 😐 ☹	☺ 😐 ☹		
I can explain the effect that ADH has on the kidneys and blood water concentration **Biology only** **Higher tier only**	☺ 😐 ☹	☺ 😐 ☹	☺ 😐 ☹		TuitionKit http://bit.ly/ 2x7DEmm

I can describe the treatment for kidney failure **Biology only**	☺ 😐 ☹	☺ 😐 ☹	☺ 😐 ☹		TuitionKit http://bit.ly/2h9ZVfD
I can describe the roles of the different hormones in the menstrual cycle	☺ 😐 ☹	☺ 😐 ☹	☺ 😐 ☹		TuitionKit http://bit.ly/2frojpb
I can describe the roles of the different hormones in puberty	☺ 😐 ☹	☺ 😐 ☹	☺ 😐 ☹		
I can describe ovulation	☺ 😐 ☹	☺ 😐 ☹	☺ 😐 ☹		
I can describe the role of testosterone	☺ 😐 ☹	☺ 😐 ☹	☺ 😐 ☹		
I can describe the interaction between FSH, LH and oestrogen in the menstrual cycle **Higher tier only**	☺ 😐 ☹	☺ 😐 ☹	☺ 😐 ☹		
I can describe different method of contraception, including hormonal and non-hormonal methods	☺ 😐 ☹	☺ 😐 ☹	☺ 😐 ☹		TuitionKit http://bit.ly/2y5Zl5u
I can explain different method of contraception, including hormonal and non-hormonal methods	☺ 😐 ☹	☺ 😐 ☹	☺ 😐 ☹		
I can describe the need for treatment for infertility **Higher tier only**	☺ 😐 ☹	☺ 😐 ☹	☺ 😐 ☹	https://youtu.be/LrwgFZaGpvY	TuitionKit http://bit.ly/2fr34nw
I can explain the process of IVF **Higher tier only**	☺ 😐 ☹	☺ 😐 ☹	☺ 😐 ☹		
I can evaluate the positive and negative effects of IVF **Higher tier only**	☺ 😐 ☹	☺ 😐 ☹	☺ 😐 ☹		
I can explain the role and regulation of thyroxine in the body **Higher tier only**	☺ 😐 ☹	☺ 😐 ☹	☺ 😐 ☹		
I can explain the role and regulation of adrenaline in the body **Higher tier only**	☺ 😐 ☹	☺ 😐 ☹	☺ 😐 ☹		
I can explain what happens in phototropism **Biology only**	☺ 😐 ☹	☺ 😐 ☹	☺ 😐 ☹		TuitionKit http://bit.ly/2jxILt1

I can explain what happens in gravitropism or geotropism **Biology only**	☺ 😐 ☹	☺ 😐 ☹	☺ 😐 ☹	https://youtu.be/ 57IXUG0CHSQ	
I can explain the role and mechanism of gibberellins **Biology only**	☺ 😐 ☹	☺ 😐 ☹	☺ 😐 ☹		TuitionKit http://bit.ly/ 2x4pp4d
I can explain the role and mechanism of ethene **Biology only**	☺ 😐 ☹	☺ 😐 ☹	☺ 😐 ☹		
I can explain the role and mechanism of auxins **Biology only** **Higher tier only**	☺ 😐 ☹	☺ 😐 ☹	☺ 😐 ☹		

Quick Fire Questions

This video is fully supported by a video tutorial; https://youtu.be/EMf0FbJI9BU

1. Define homoeostasis.
2. What does the brain do in homeostasis?
3. What does central nervous system do in homeostasis?
4. What is the endocrine system?
5. Where is the pituitary gland?
6. Where is the pancreas?
7. Where is the thyroid?
8. Where is the adrenal gland?
9. Where are the ovaries?
10. Where are the testis?
11. How is blood glucose monitored?
12. What happens when blood glucose is too high?
13. What is the menstrual cycle?
14. What is ovulation?
15. What is testosterone?
16. What is contraception?

Higher tier only

17. What happens when blood glucose is too low?
18. What is a negative feedback loop?
19. What is FSH?
20. What is LH?
21. What is oestrogen?
22. Where is FSH produced?
23. Where does FSH act?
24. Where is LH produced?
25. Where does LH act?
26. Where is oestrogen produced?
27. Where does oestrogen act?
28. What is IVF?
29. Give two positives about IVF?
30. Give two negatives about IVF?
31. What is thyroxine?
32. Where is thyroxine produced?
33. Where does thyroxine act?
34. What is adrenaline?

35. Where is adrenaline produced?
36. Where does adrenaline act?

Biology Only

37. Label these different parts of the brain.

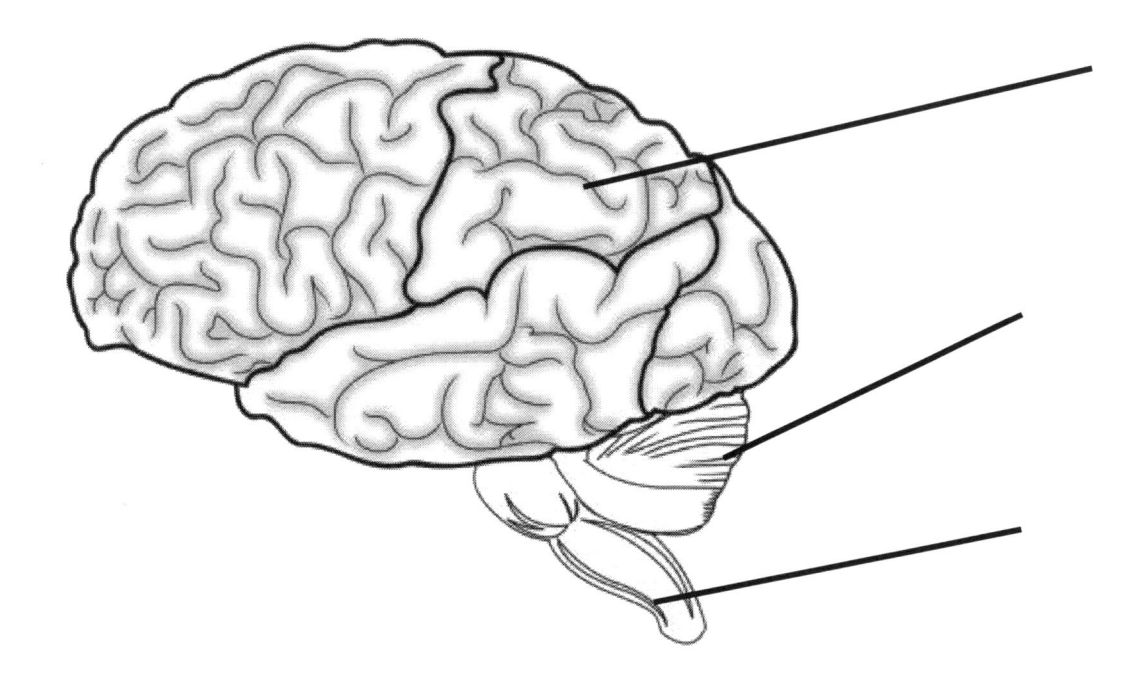

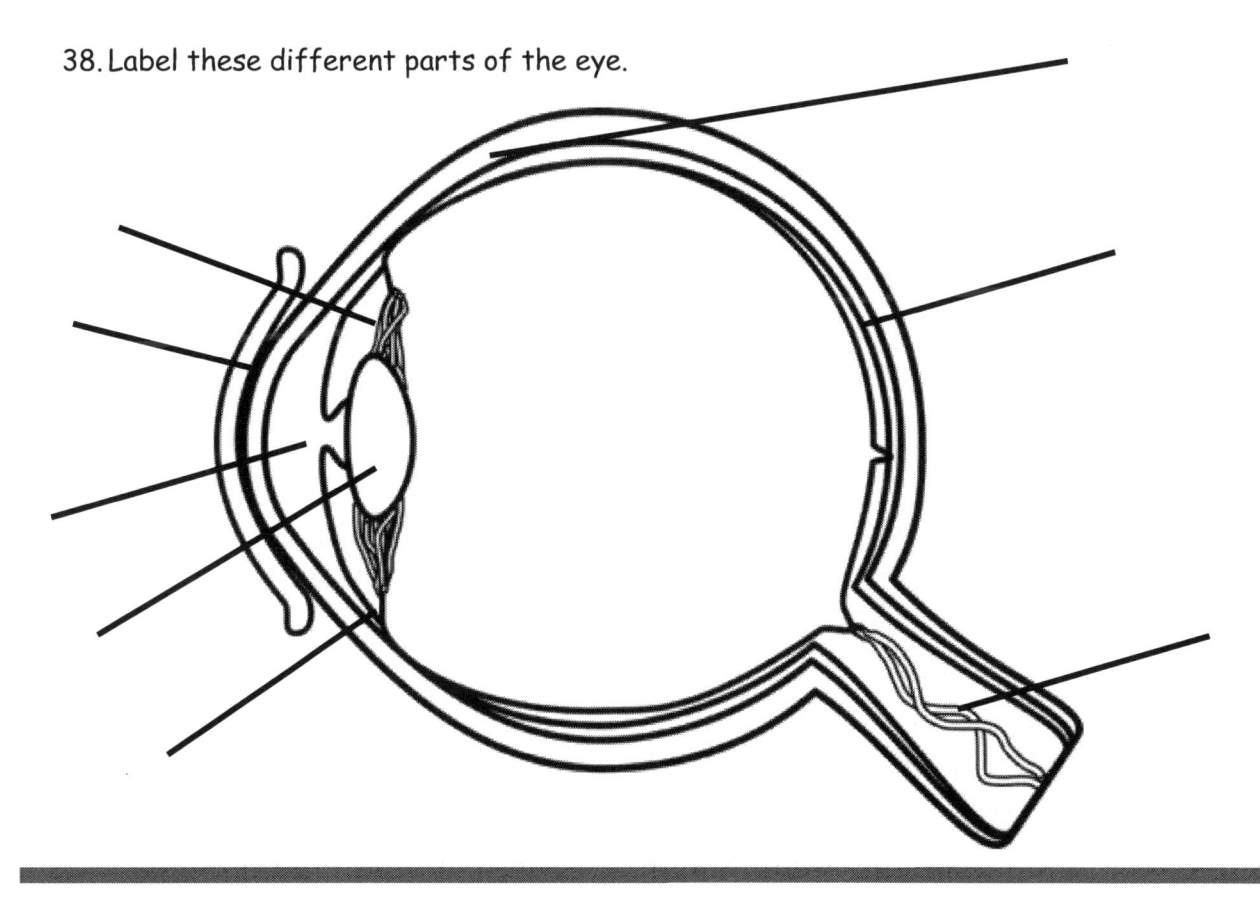

38. Label these different parts of the eye.

39. What is short-sightedness?
40. What is long-sightedness?
41. How can short-sightedness be corrected?
42. How can long-sightedness be corrected?
43. What is osmosis?
44. How does water leave the body?
45. How does water get into the body?
46. What happens to cells if they lose too much water?
47. What happens to cells if there is too much water?
48. What do the kidneys do?
49. What is the treatment for kidney failure?
50. What is phototropism?
51. What is geotropism?
52. What is the role of gibberellins?
53. What does ADH stand for?
54. What does ADHD do?

6 – Inheritance, variation and evolution

Knowledge Checklist

Specification statement — These are the bits the exam board wants you to know, make sure you can do all of these…	Self-assessment			Bits to help if you don't understand	
	First review 4-7 months before exam	Second review 1-2 months before exam	Final review Week before exam	Primrose Kitten	Other places
I can describe the differences in the end result of mitosis and meiosis	☺ 😐 ☹	☺ 😐 ☹	☺ 😐 ☹	https://youtu.be/pi6sbTc4wBo	TuitionKit http://bit.ly/2f2e2PA
I can recall the names of the male and female gametes in plants and animals	☺ 😐 ☹	☺ 😐 ☹	☺ 😐 ☹		
I can describe the process of meiosis	☺ 😐 ☹	☺ 😐 ☹	☺ 😐 ☹	https://youtu.be/pi6sbTc4wBo	TuitionKit http://bit.ly/2f2e2PA
I can describe the process of asexual reproduction	☺ 😐 ☹	☺ 😐 ☹	☺ 😐 ☹		
I can describe the advantages and disadvantages of sexual and asexual reproduction **Biology only**	☺ 😐 ☹	☺ 😐 ☹	☺ 😐 ☹		TuitionKit http://bit.ly/2f21ojx
I can describe the structure of DNA	☺ 😐 ☹	☺ 😐 ☹	☺ 😐 ☹	https://youtu.be/erZB_EhuKbA	
I can describe the structure of a chromosome	☺ 😐 ☹	☺ 😐 ☹	☺ 😐 ☹		
I can define the term gene	☺ 😐 ☹	☺ 😐 ☹	☺ 😐 ☹		
I can define the term genome	☺ 😐 ☹	☺ 😐 ☹	☺ 😐 ☹		
I can describe the structure of DNA including the nucleotide, sugar and phosphate groups **Biology only**	☺ 😐 ☹	☺ 😐 ☹	☺ 😐 ☹	https://youtu.be/erZB_EhuKbA	
I can recall the different bases in DNA **Biology only**	☺ 😐 ☹	☺ 😐 ☹	☺ 😐 ☹		

I can describe how different sequences of DNA code for amino acids **Biology only**	☺ 😐 ☹	☺ 😐 ☹	☺ 😐 ☹		
I can describe the process of protein synthesis **Biology only** **Higher tier only**	☺ 😐 ☹	☺ 😐 ☹	☺ 😐 ☹		
I can describe how variations in DNA can affect the protein being made **Biology only** **Higher tier only**	☺ 😐 ☹	☺ 😐 ☹	☺ 😐 ☹		
I can recall that the bases C and G match up and the bases A and T match up **Biology only** **Higher tier only**	☺ 😐 ☹	☺ 😐 ☹	☺ 😐 ☹		
I can describe the process of protein synthesis **Biology only** **Higher tier only**	☺ 😐 ☹	☺ 😐 ☹	☺ 😐 ☹		
I can describe the process of protein folding **Biology only** **Higher tier only**	☺ 😐 ☹	☺ 😐 ☹	☺ 😐 ☹		
I can describe the effect a mutation can have on a protein **Biology only** **Higher tier only**	☺ 😐 ☹	☺ 😐 ☹	☺ 😐 ☹		
I can describe the effect a mutation can have on an enzyme **Biology only** **Higher tier only**	☺ 😐 ☹	☺ 😐 ☹	☺ 😐 ☹		
I can explain non-coding DNA **Biology only** **Higher tier only**	☺ 😐 ☹	☺ 😐 ☹	☺ 😐 ☹		
I can define the term gamete	☺ 😐 ☹	☺ 😐 ☹	☺ 😐 ☹		
I can define the term chromosome	☺ 😐 ☹	☺ 😐 ☹	☺ 😐 ☹		
I can define the term gene	☺ 😐 ☹	☺ 😐 ☹	☺ 😐 ☹		
I can define the term allele	☺ 😐 ☹	☺ 😐 ☹	☺ 😐 ☹		
I can define the term dominant	☺ 😐 ☹	☺ 😐 ☹	☺ 😐 ☹		

I can define the term recessive	☺ 😐 ☹	☺ 😐 ☹	☺ 😐 ☹	
I can define the term homozygous	☺ 😐 ☹	☺ 😐 ☹	☺ 😐 ☹	
I can define the term heterozygous	☺ 😐 ☹	☺ 😐 ☹	☺ 😐 ☹	
I can define the term genotype	☺ 😐 ☹	☺ 😐 ☹	☺ 😐 ☹	
I can define the term phenotype	☺ 😐 ☹	☺ 😐 ☹	☺ 😐 ☹	
I can explain how characteristic can be controlled by genes	☺ 😐 ☹	☺ 😐 ☹	☺ 😐 ☹	
I can predict the results of a genetic cross by completing a Punnett square diagram	☺ 😐 ☹	☺ 😐 ☹	☺ 😐 ☹	
I can describe the phenotype and genotype of a person with polydactyly	☺ 😐 ☹	☺ 😐 ☹	☺ 😐 ☹	
I can describe the phenotype and genotype of a person with cystic fibrosis	☺ 😐 ☹	☺ 😐 ☹	☺ 😐 ☹	
I can make an informed judgement about embryo screening	☺ 😐 ☹	☺ 😐 ☹	☺ 😐 ☹	
I can recall the number of pairs of chromosomes in a human body cell	☺ 😐 ☹	☺ 😐 ☹	☺ 😐 ☹	
I can recall that sex is determine by the X and Y chromosomes	☺ 😐 ☹	☺ 😐 ☹	☺ 😐 ☹	
I can describe how phenotype can be influenced by genes and the environment	☺ 😐 ☹	☺ 😐 ☹	☺ 😐 ☹	
I can recall that difference in a population in variation	☺ 😐 ☹	☺ 😐 ☹	☺ 😐 ☹	
I can describe the factors that affect variation within a population	☺ 😐 ☹	☺ 😐 ☹	☺ 😐 ☹	
I can recall that mutations continuously occur	☺ 😐 ☹	☺ 😐 ☹	☺ 😐 ☹	
I can define evolution	☺ 😐 ☹	☺ 😐 ☹	☺ 😐 ☹	TuitionKit http://bit.ly/2h90Clx
I can describe the theory of evolution	☺ 😐 ☹	☺ 😐 ☹	☺ 😐 ☹	
I can explain natural selection	☺ 😐 ☹	☺ 😐 ☹	☺ 😐 ☹	
I can explain speciation	☺ 😐 ☹	☺ 😐 ☹	☺ 😐 ☹	

I can describe the impact of selective breading	☺ 😐 ☹	☺ 😐 ☹	☺ 😐 ☹		
I can define the term genetic engineering	☺ 😐 ☹	☺ 😐 ☹	☺ 😐 ☹		
I can describe the use of genetic engineering in plants	☺ 😐 ☹	☺ 😐 ☹	☺ 😐 ☹		
I can describe the use of genetically engineered bacteria to produce insulin.	☺ 😐 ☹	☺ 😐 ☹	☺ 😐 ☹		
I can evaluate the advantages and disadvantages of genetic engineering in agriculture	☺ 😐 ☹	☺ 😐 ☹	☺ 😐 ☹		
I can describe the process of producing a genetically modified crop	☺ 😐 ☹	☺ 😐 ☹	☺ 😐 ☹		
I can explain the potential for genetic modification to treat inherited disorders	☺ 😐 ☹	☺ 😐 ☹	☺ 😐 ☹		
I can explain the process of producing a genetically modified crop **Higher tier only**	☺ 😐 ☹	☺ 😐 ☹	☺ 😐 ☹		
I can describe the process of cloning via cuttings **Biology only**	☺ 😐 ☹	☺ 😐 ☹	☺ 😐 ☹		
I can describe the process of cloning via tissue culture **Biology only**	☺ 😐 ☹	☺ 😐 ☹	☺ 😐 ☹		
I can describe the process of cloning via embryo transplant **Biology only**	☺ 😐 ☹	☺ 😐 ☹	☺ 😐 ☹		
I can describe the process of cloning via adult cell cloning **Biology only**	☺ 😐 ☹	☺ 😐 ☹	☺ 😐 ☹		
I can explain how Darwin came to propose the theory of evolution **Biology only**	☺ 😐 ☹	☺ 😐 ☹	☺ 😐 ☹		
I can explain the theory of evolution **Biology only**	☺ 😐 ☹	☺ 😐 ☹	☺ 😐 ☹		TuitionKit http://bit.ly/2h9OClx

I can discuss the controversy around Darwin's ideas when they were published **Biology only**	☺ ☻ ☹	☺ ☻ ☹	☺ ☻ ☹		
I can discuss other theories of evolution, such as Lamarck's ideas **Biology only**	☺ ☻ ☹	☺ ☻ ☹	☺ ☻ ☹		
I can define the term speciation **Biology only**	☺ ☻ ☹	☺ ☻ ☹	☺ ☻ ☹		
I can describe Wallace's theory of evolution **Biology only**	☺ ☻ ☹	☺ ☻ ☹	☺ ☻ ☹		
I can describe the steps that lead to a new species **Biology only**	☺ ☻ ☹	☺ ☻ ☹	☺ ☻ ☹		
I can describe the work that Mendel did **Biology only**	☺ ☻ ☹	☺ ☻ ☹	☺ ☻ ☹		
I can explain the evidence for evolution	☺ ☻ ☹	☺ ☻ ☹	☺ ☻ ☹		
I can describe how fossils arise	☺ ☻ ☹	☺ ☻ ☹	☺ ☻ ☹		TuitionKit http://bit.ly/2xb1tLU
I can explain why not all organism leave fossils	☺ ☻ ☹	☺ ☻ ☹	☺ ☻ ☹		
I can describe what fossils teach us	☺ ☻ ☹	☺ ☻ ☹	☺ ☻ ☹		
I can use an evolutionary tree	☺ ☻ ☹	☺ ☻ ☹	☺ ☻ ☹	https://youtu.be/rTHVPh1kO5o	https://phet.colorado.edu/en/simulation/natural-selection
I can define the term extinction	☺ ☻ ☹	☺ ☻ ☹	☺ ☻ ☹		
I can describe the factors that lead to an extinction	☺ ☻ ☹	☺ ☻ ☹	☺ ☻ ☹		
I can explain why bacteria can evolve quickly	☺ ☻ ☹	☺ ☻ ☹	☺ ☻ ☹		
I can describe why antibiotic resistance could arise	☺ ☻ ☹	☺ ☻ ☹	☺ ☻ ☹		
I can describe the effect of MRSA (and other antibiotic resistance strains of bacteria) have on humans	☺ ☻ ☹	☺ ☻ ☹	☺ ☻ ☹		

I can describe why the development of new antibiotics is slow	☺ 😐 ☹	☺ 😐 ☹	☺ 😐 ☹		
I can describe the system of classification that Linnaeus developed	☺ 😐 ☹	☺ 😐 ☹	☺ 😐 ☹		
I can determine an organism's genus and species from a tree	☺ 😐 ☹	☺ 😐 ☹	☺ 😐 ☹		
I can describe how developments in biology can impact on classification	☺ 😐 ☹	☺ 😐 ☹	☺ 😐 ☹		
I can describe the 'three domain system' of archaea, bacteria and eukaryote	☺ 😐 ☹	☺ 😐 ☹	☺ 😐 ☹		

Quick Fire Questions

This worksheet is fully supported by a video tutorial; https://youtu.be/IL-dUnKmksY

1. How many cells are produced at the end of mitosis?
2. How many cells are produced at the end of meiosis?
3. What are the male gametes in plants?
4. What the female gametes in plants?
5. What are the male gametes in animals?
6. What are the female gametes in animals?
7. What is the basic structure of DNA?
8. Define gene.
9. Define genome.
10. Define gamete.
11. Define chromosome.
12. Define allele.
13. Define dominant.
14. Define recessive.
15. Define homozygous.
16. Define heterozygous.
17. Defined genotype.
18. Define phenotype.
19. What is polydactyly?
20. Is polydactyly dominant or recessive?
21. What is cystic fibrosis?
22. Is cystic fibrosis dominant or recessive?
23. How many pairs of chromosomes in human body cell?
24. What sex is XX?
25. What sex is XY?
26. Define evolution.
27. Define natural selection.
28. Despite the speciation.
29. What evidence is there for evolution?
30. How do fossils arise?
31. Define extinction.
32. What things lead to extinction?
33. Why can bacteria evolve quickly?
34. What is MRSA?
35. Why is the development of antibiotics so slow?

Biology only

36. What are the advantages of sexual reproduction?
37. With the disadvantages of sexual production?
38. What are the advantages of asexual reproduction?
39. What are the disadvantages of asexual reproduction?
40. What is the basic structure of DNA?
41. What are the bases in DNA?
42. How does DNA code for amino acids?
43. How do amino acids produce proteins?
44. How do variations in DNA affect the protein being made?
45. What affect might a mutation have on an enzyme?
46. What was Darwin's theory?
47. What was the controversy behind Darwin's theory?
48. What was the Lamarck's theory?

7 – Ecology

Knowledge Checklist

| Specification statement

These are the bits the exam board wants you to know, make sure you can do all of these...	Self-assessment			Bits to help if you don't understand	
	First review 4-7 months before exam	Second review 1-2 months before exam	Final review Week before exam	Primrose Kitten	Other places
I can describe the levels of organisation in an ecosystem	☺ ☺ ☹	☺ ☺ ☹	☺ ☺ ☹		
I can define the term community	☺ ☺ ☹	☺ ☺ ☹	☺ ☺ ☹		
I can describe interdependence in a community	☺ ☺ ☹	☺ ☺ ☹	☺ ☺ ☹		
I can describe competition in a community	☺ ☺ ☹	☺ ☺ ☹	☺ ☺ ☹		
I can define the term ecosystem	☺ ☺ ☹	☺ ☺ ☹	☺ ☺ ☹		
I can describe what an organism needs to survive and reproduce	☺ ☺ ☹	☺ ☺ ☹	☺ ☺ ☹		
I can describe what different organisms compete for	☺ ☺ ☹	☺ ☺ ☹	☺ ☺ ☹		
I can define the term abiotic factor	☺ ☺ ☹	☺ ☺ ☹	☺ ☺ ☹		
I can recall a list of abiotic factors including; light intensity, temperature, water levels, pH, ion content, wind, carbon dioxide and oxygen levels	☺ ☺ ☹	☺ ☺ ☹	☺ ☺ ☹		
I can describe how a change in abiotic factors could affect a community	☺ ☺ ☹	☺ ☺ ☹	☺ ☺ ☹		
I can define the term biotic factor	☺ ☺ ☹	☺ ☺ ☹	☺ ☺ ☹		
I can describe how a change in biotic factors could affect a community	☺ ☺ ☹	☺ ☺ ☹	☺ ☺ ☹		

I can recall a list of biotic factors including; food, predators and pathogens.	☺ 😐 ☹	☺ 😐 ☹	☺ 😐 ☹		
I can define the term adaptation	☺ 😐 ☹	☺ 😐 ☹	☺ 😐 ☹		
I can describe why animals and plants need adaptations	☺ 😐 ☹	☺ 😐 ☹	☺ 😐 ☹		
I can define the term extremophile	☺ 😐 ☹	☺ 😐 ☹	☺ 😐 ☹		
I can give examples of plant and animal adaptations	☺ 😐 ☹	☺ 😐 ☹	☺ 😐 ☹		
I can describe where the biomass on Earth comes from	☺ 😐 ☹	☺ 😐 ☹	☺ 😐 ☹		
I can draw a food chain	☺ 😐 ☹	☺ 😐 ☹	☺ 😐 ☹		
I can explain where the energy is a food chain comes from	☺ 😐 ☹	☺ 😐 ☹	☺ 😐 ☹		
I can describe how to use a quadrate	☺ 😐 ☹	☺ 😐 ☹	☺ 😐 ☹		
I can describe how to use a transect	☺ 😐 ☹	☺ 😐 ☹	☺ 😐 ☹		
I can describe how to determine the abundance and distribution of species in an ecosystem	☺ 😐 ☹	☺ 😐 ☹	☺ 😐 ☹		
I can define the term producer	☺ 😐 ☹	☺ 😐 ☹	☺ 😐 ☹		
I can define the term primary consumer	☺ 😐 ☹	☺ 😐 ☹	☺ 😐 ☹		
I can define the term secondary consumer	☺ 😐 ☹	☺ 😐 ☹	☺ 😐 ☹		
I can define the term tertiary consumer	☺ 😐 ☹	☺ 😐 ☹	☺ 😐 ☹		
I can define the term prey	☺ 😐 ☹	☺ 😐 ☹	☺ 😐 ☹		
I can describe the carbon cycle	☺ 😐 ☹	☺ 😐 ☹	☺ 😐 ☹	https://youtu.be/Uoqp7QjWW-M	
I can describe the water cycle	☺ 😐 ☹	☺ 😐 ☹	☺ 😐 ☹		
I can recall that materials are recycled through biotic and abiotic part of an ecosystem and provide building blocks for the future.	☺ 😐 ☹	☺ 😐 ☹	☺ 😐 ☹		
I can describe the role of microorganisms in cycling materials	☺ 😐 ☹	☺ 😐 ☹	☺ 😐 ☹		

I can define the terms decay and decomposition **Biology only**	☺ 😐 ☹	☺ 😐 ☹	☺ 😐 ☹		
I can describe how differences in temperature can affect the rate of decomposition **Biology only**	☺ 😐 ☹	☺ 😐 ☹	☺ 😐 ☹		
I can describe how differences in oxygen can affect the rate of decomposition **Biology only**	☺ 😐 ☹	☺ 😐 ☹	☺ 😐 ☹		
I can describe how differences in water can affect the rate of decomposition **Biology only**	☺ 😐 ☹	☺ 😐 ☹	☺ 😐 ☹		
I can explain why gardeners compost **Biology only**	☺ 😐 ☹	☺ 😐 ☹	☺ 😐 ☹		
I can describe how decay can lead to the production of biogas **Biology only**	☺ 😐 ☹	☺ 😐 ☹	☺ 😐 ☹		
I can evaluate the impact of environmental changes (including temperature, water and the atmosphere) on the distribution of a species **Biology only**	☺ 😐 ☹	☺ 😐 ☹	☺ 😐 ☹		TuitionKit http://bit.ly/2yfsyvO
I can define the term biodiversity	☺ 😐 ☹	☺ 😐 ☹	☺ 😐 ☹		TuitionKit http://bit.ly/2xpTFpN
I can explain the needs for biodiversity	☺ 😐 ☹	☺ 😐 ☹	☺ 😐 ☹		
I can describe the impact that humans have on biodiversity	☺ 😐 ☹	☺ 😐 ☹	☺ 😐 ☹		
I can explain the rise in pollution	☺ 😐 ☹	☺ 😐 ☹	☺ 😐 ☹		
I can describe the range of different sources of pollution, including; in water, in air and in land	☺ 😐 ☹	☺ 😐 ☹	☺ 😐 ☹		TuitionKit http://bit.ly/2f2cbdE
I can describe the effect that pollution has of plants and animals	☺ 😐 ☹	☺ 😐 ☹	☺ 😐 ☹		
I can describe the impact that humans have on land use and the effect this has on plant and animal life	☺ 😐 ☹	☺ 😐 ☹	☺ 😐 ☹		TuitionKit http://bit.ly/2h6qsdE

I can describe the impact of the destruction of peat bogs	☺ ☻ ☹	☺ ☻ ☹	☺ ☻ ☹		
I can describe the impact of deforestation	☺ ☻ ☹	☺ ☻ ☹	☺ ☻ ☹		TuitionKit http://bit.ly/2h71jzj
I can recall the reasons for deforestation	☺ ☻ ☹	☺ ☻ ☹	☺ ☻ ☹		
I can describe the biological consequences of global warming	☺ ☻ ☹	☺ ☻ ☹	☺ ☻ ☹		TuitionKit http://bit.ly/2xaBX9x
I can recall the gases that contribute to global warming	☺ ☻ ☹	☺ ☻ ☹	☺ ☻ ☹	https://youtu.be/y5PZ1RN5mt0	
I can describe how humans can have a positive and a negative impact on biodiversity	☺ ☻ ☹	☺ ☻ ☹	☺ ☻ ☹		
I can discuss the range of programmes that aim to reduce the negative effect of humans on biodiversity	☺ ☻ ☹	☺ ☻ ☹	☺ ☻ ☹		
I can define the term trophic level **Biology only**	☺ ☻ ☹	☺ ☻ ☹	☺ ☻ ☹		
I can use number to represent trophic levels **Biology only**	☺ ☻ ☹	☺ ☻ ☹	☺ ☻ ☹		
I can describe the differences between the trophic levels **Biology only**	☺ ☻ ☹	☺ ☻ ☹	☺ ☻ ☹		
I can describe the role of decomposers **Biology only**	☺ ☻ ☹	☺ ☻ ☹	☺ ☻ ☹		
I can construct a pyramid of biomass **Biology only**	☺ ☻ ☹	☺ ☻ ☹	☺ ☻ ☹		
I can interpret a pyramid of biomass **Biology only**	☺ ☻ ☹	☺ ☻ ☹	☺ ☻ ☹		
I can explain how energy is lost between trophic levels **Biology only**	☺ ☻ ☹	☺ ☻ ☹	☺ ☻ ☹		
I can recall that roughly 10% of the energy is transferred to the next trophic level **Biology only**	☺ ☻ ☹	☺ ☻ ☹	☺ ☻ ☹		

I can define the term food security **Biology only**	☺ 😐 ☹	☺ 😐 ☹	☺ 😐 ☹		TuitionKit http://bit.ly/2y5FraQ
I can explain the factors affecting food security **Biology only**	☺ 😐 ☹	☺ 😐 ☹	☺ 😐 ☹		
I can describe the need to find sustainable methods for food production **Biology only**	☺ 😐 ☹	☺ 😐 ☹	☺ 😐 ☹		
I can describe ways to improve the efficiency of food production **Biology only**	☺ 😐 ☹	☺ 😐 ☹	☺ 😐 ☹		
I can describe why some farmers use high protein foods **Biology only**	☺ 😐 ☹	☺ 😐 ☹	☺ 😐 ☹		TuitionKit http://bit.ly/2x4Yq8I
I can describe the need for sustainable fisheries **Biology only**	☺ 😐 ☹	☺ 😐 ☹	☺ 😐 ☹		TuitionKit http://bit.ly/2yf2l0f
I can explain the methods used to keep fish stocks at a sustainable level **Biology only**	☺ 😐 ☹	☺ 😐 ☹	☺ 😐 ☹		
I can describe the advances in biotechnology as they apply to agriculture **Biology only**	☺ 😐 ☹	☺ 😐 ☹	☺ 😐 ☹		TuitionKit http://bit.ly/2xHnALf
I can describe that microorganism can be cultured for food **Biology only**	☺ 😐 ☹	☺ 😐 ☹	☺ 😐 ☹		

Quick fire Questions

This worksheet is fully supported by a video tutorial; https://youtu.be/NorHSgd7Yyc

1. Define ecosystem.
2. Define community.
3. Define interdependence.
4. Define competition.
5. What does an organism need to survive and reproduce?
6. What do different organisms compete for?
7. Define abiotic factor.
8. List eight abiotic factors.
9. How can a change in abiotic factors affect the community?
10. Define biotic factors.
11. How can a change in biotic factors affect the community?
12. List three biotic factors.
13. Define adaptation.
14. Why do animals need to adapt?
15. Define extremophile.
16. Give an example of a plant adaptation.
17. Give an example of an animal adaptation.
18. Where does energy in a food chain come from?
19. Define the term producer.
20. Define the term primary consumer.
21. Define the term secondary consumer.
22. Define the term tertiary consumer.
23. Define the term prey.
24. Define the term biodiversity.
25. Why do we need biodiversity?
26. What is pollution?
27. What impact can pollution have on plants?
28. What impact can pollution have on animals?
29. What impact can humans have on land usage?
30. What is the impact of deforestation?
31. What are the reasons for deforestation?
32. What the consequences of global warming?
33. What gases contribute to global warming?

Biology only

34. Define the term decay.
35. Define the term decomposition.
36. How can temperature affect the rate of decomposition?
37. How can oxygen affect the rate of decomposition?
38. How can water affect the rate of decomposition?
39. How can decay lead to the production of biogas?
40. Define the term biodiversity.
41. What is the differences between trophic levels?
42. What is the role of a decomposer?
43. How is energy lost between trophic levels?
44. What is food security?
45. How can we increase efficiency of the production?
46. How can microorganisms be cultured for food?

Crosswords

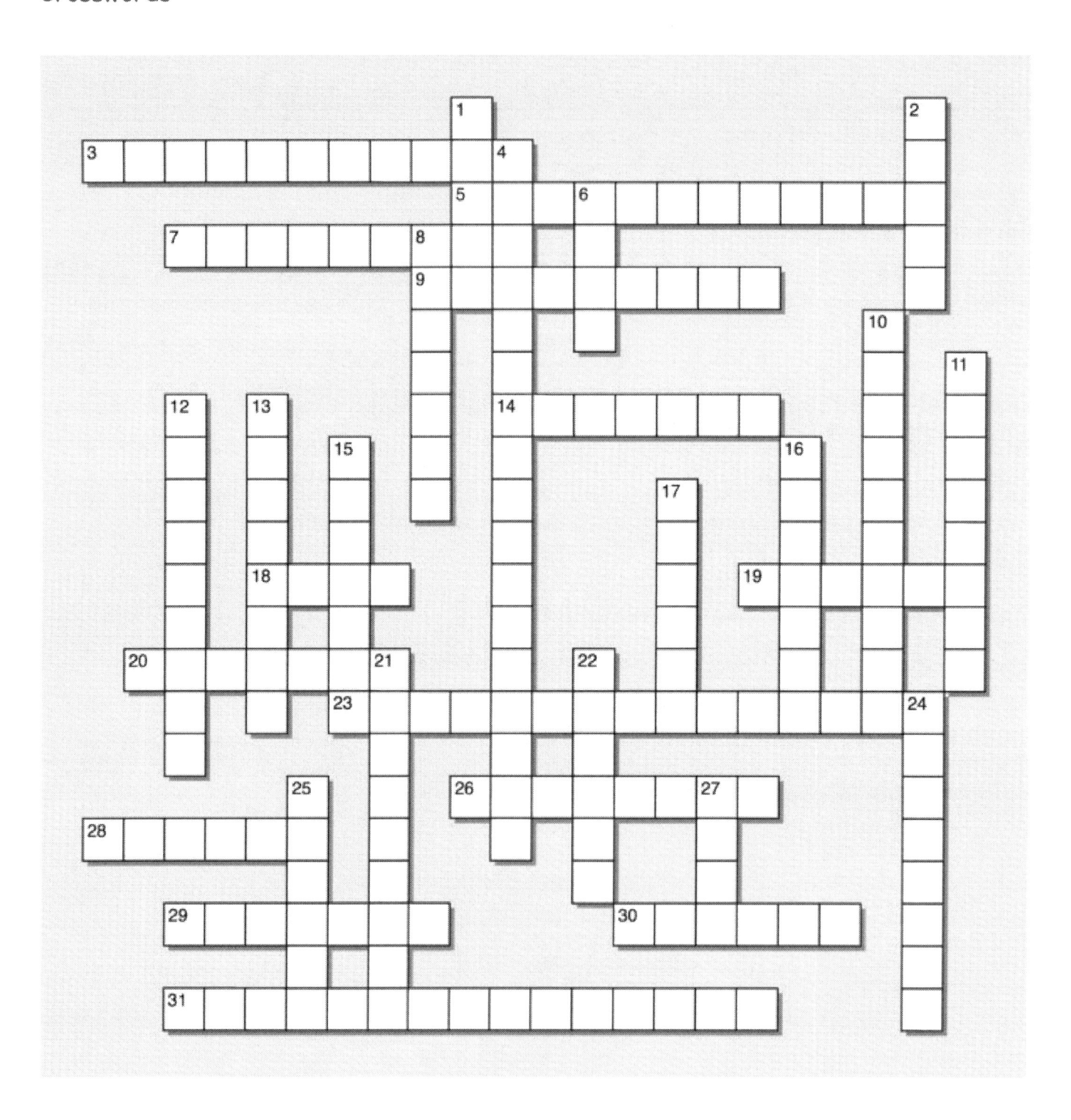

Across

3) lump of cells that are not invading the body

5) carries oxygen around the body, has no nucleus

7) small fragments of blood cells that help clotting

9) Thinned walled blood vessels that allow diffusion of gases and nutrients

14) Enzyme that breaks carbohydrates into sugars

18) Small structural unit that contains a nucleus and cytoplasm

19) fluid part of the blood

20) one copy of each chromosome

23) organ system that absorbs nutrients from food

26) Major blood vessel that carries deoxygenated blood back to the heart

28) state of mental and physical wellbeing

29) Type of cell division that ends in two identical daughter cells

30) uncontrolled cell division within the body

31) Blood vessel that carries deoxygenated blood from the heart to the lungs

Down

1) Major blood vessel that carries oxygenated blood away from the heart

2) carries water around a plant

4) organ system that moves oxygen around the body

6) Produced by the liver, neutralizes stomach acid and emulsifies fats

8) the study of organism within and environment

10) long stretch of DNA

11) Enzyme that breaks proteins into amino acids

12) jelly like substance within a cell

13) a type of cell that can differentiate into any other type of cell

15) two copies of each chromosome

16) control centre of the cell, that holds the DNA

17) Biological catalyst

21) movement of ions or gasses from a high concentration to a low concentration

22) Enzyme that breaks fats into fatty acids and glycerol

24) plant tissue found at growing tips

25) carries ions around a plant

27) Blood vessels that have values and carries deoxygenated blood back to the heart

Biology Crossword 2

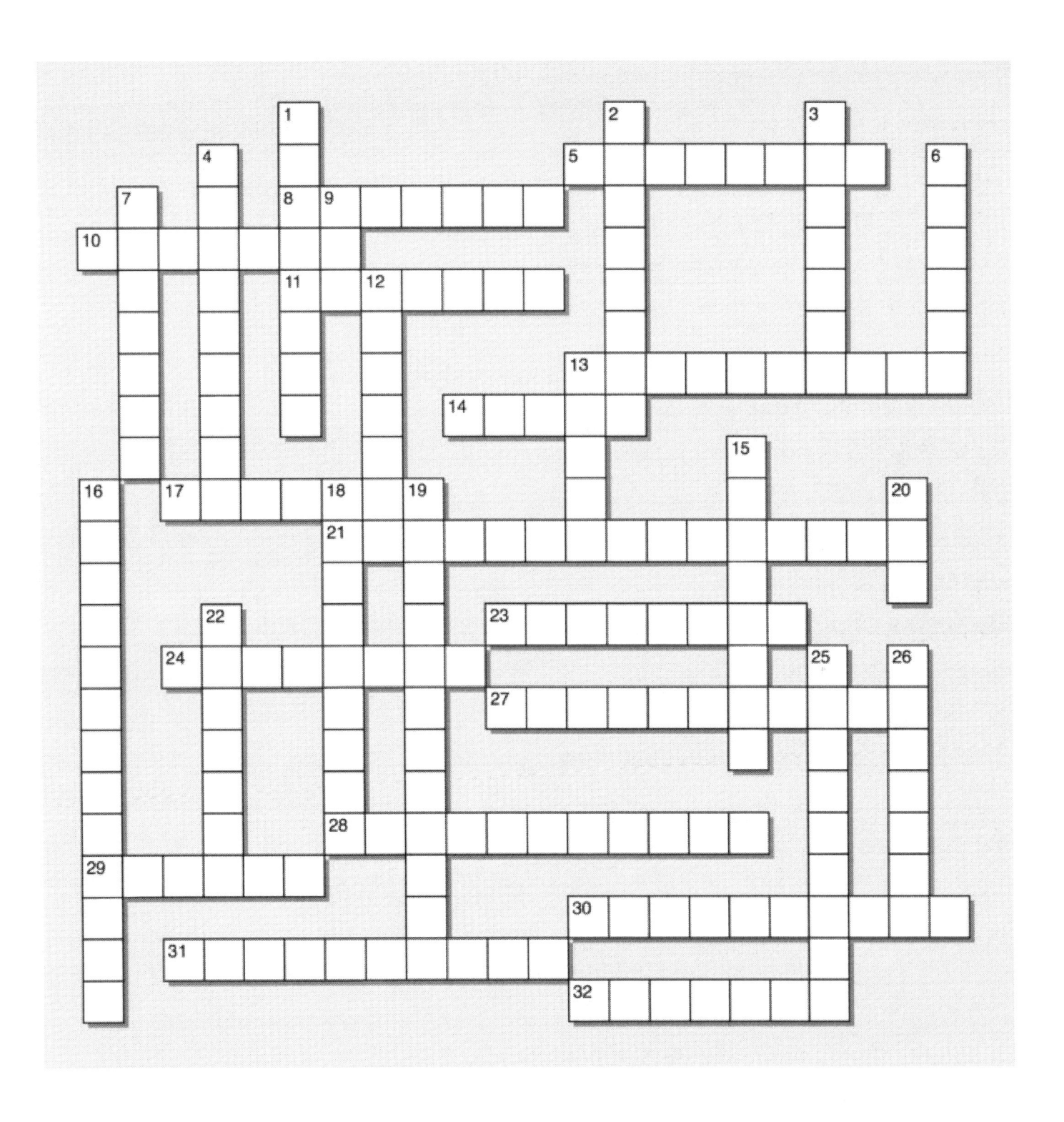

Across

5) medication that contain inactive or dead virus to help develop immunity

8) large gland in the neck which releases hormone

10) braches of the trachea

11) in women, these store the eggs

13) can be combined with glycerol to make lipids

14) DNA within a protein coat that divides by invading cells, the resulting cell death causes illness in the host

17) parasite transmitted by mosquitoes

21) system that controls hormones and responses

23) inability of the bod to control blood glucose levels

24) long chains of amino acids, that carry out the majority of functions within the body

27) drugs that kill bacteria

28) green part of a plant

29) in men, these are responsible for the production of sperm

30) chemical process that occur to maintain life

31) arises after anaerobic respiration, needs oxygen to repay

32) viral infection causing fever and rash, most common in children

Down

1) causes illness

2) large gland behind the stomach which produces digestive enzymes

3) respiration with oxygen

4) bacteria that cause a sexual transmitted disease causing smelly discharge from the penis or vagina

6) stores of energy that can be broken down to form fatty acids and glycerol

7) long tube taking air down into the lungs

9) virus that interfere with your body's ability to fight disease

12) painkiller developed from willow bark

13) group that includes mushrooms and moulds, they live of decomposing material

15) can be combined with fatty acid to make lipids

16) process where plant absorb and lose water

18) nerve pathway including a sensory nerve a synapse and a motor nerve

19) large gland near the kidneys that releases hormone

20) virus affecting plants causing a mosaic pattern on leaves

22) tiny single celled organism that can cause illness

25) heart drug that comes from Foxglove plants

26) transport of water across a partially permeable membrane

Biology Crossword 3

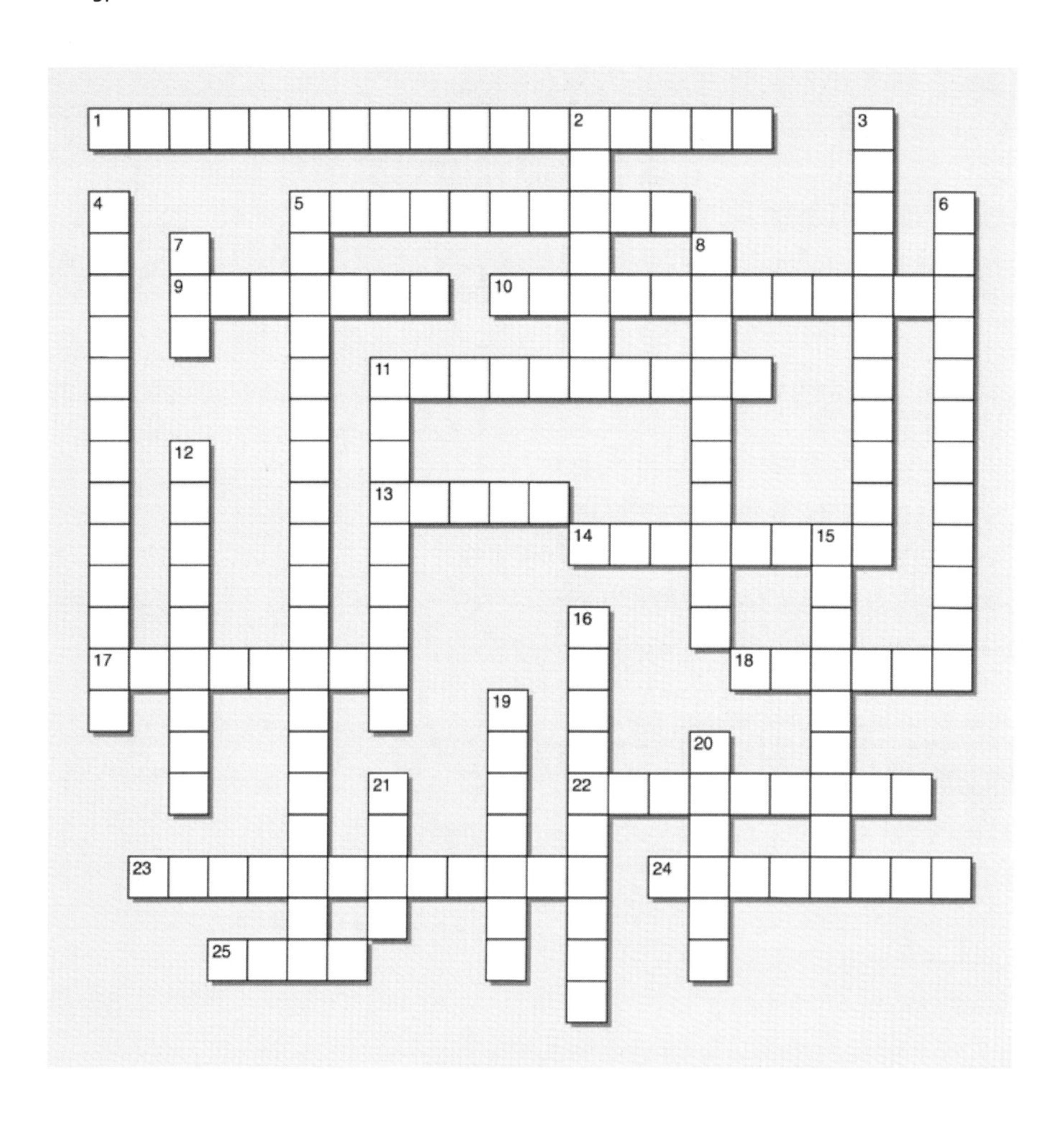

Across

1) breading of animals or plants for a particular characteristic

5) change in a species to suit the environment

9) sex cells

10) different copies of gene

11) no breading pair of a species exist

13) male sex cell

14) what genes are present

17) eat plants and animals

18) different version of gene

22) two identical copies of the gene are needed to be expressed

23) the range of different organism that live in an environment

24) only one copy of the gene is needed to be expressed

25) section of DNA, that controls a characteristic

Down

2) non-living factors that affect organism

3) the movement of carbon through the environment

4) mechanism to prevent pregnancy

5) reproduction with only one parent, resulting in identical offspring

6) hormone found predominantly in men

7) female sex cell

8) identical copies of gene

11) the organism and the habitat they live in

12) the organism that live in a particular environment

15) harmful substance in an environment

16) the movement of water through eh environment

19) hard parts of long dead organism

20) all of the genes in an organism

21) something that gets eaten

PATREON

Join my lovely, friendly community over at
https://www.patreon.com/PrimroseKitten

- Find out what happens behind the scenes
- Get a first look at new videos
- Get advanced copies of sheets and books
- Spread out your revision and get sent flash cards and predicted papers each month

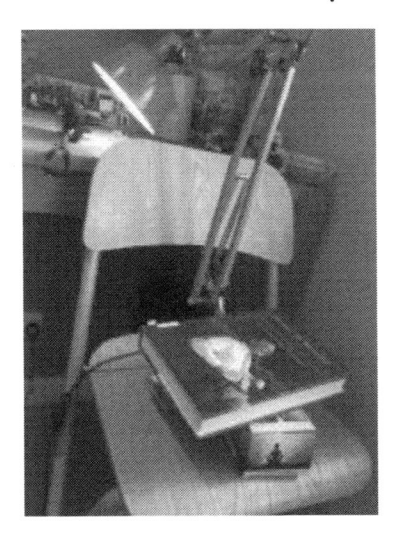

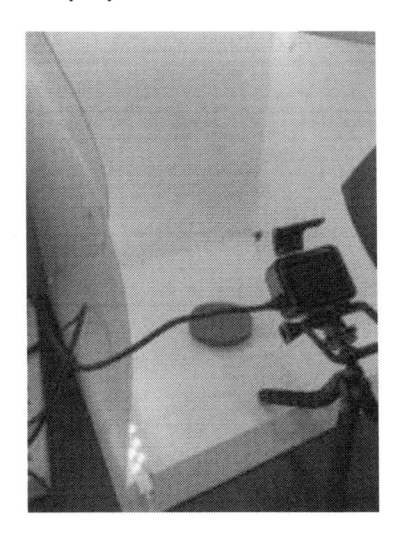

Chemistry

5 most common mistakes in a chemistry exam

1. Drawing the wrong number of bonds in organic chemistry
2. Being too wishy washy in colour changes
3. Putting numbers in the wrong place
4. Missing out (or adding in too many) capital letters
5. Keep numbers in your calculator memory to avoid rounding errors

Important tips

- When balancing equations, if you really, really can't work it out. Write 2 as the answer
- If you've forgotten the reaction conditions, write 'hot and a catalyst'

Topic Guide

Topic	First review	Second review	Third review
1 – Atomic Structure and the Periodic Table			
2 – Bonding, Structure and the Properties of Matter			
3 – Quantitative Chemistry			
4 – Chemical Changes			
5 – Energy Changes			
6 – The Rate and Extent of Chemical Change			
7 – Organic Chemistry			
8 – Chemical Analysis			
9 – Chemistry of the Atmosphere			
10 – Using Resources			

Topic	Quick fire questions	Whole topic video
1 – Atomic Structure and the Periodic Table	https://youtu.be/mjlIPJ_c018	
2 – Bonding, Structure and the Properties of Matter	https://youtu.be/9bbCFUyluWg	
3 – Quantitative Chemistry	https://youtu.be/8ugWdmIKd7c	
4 – Chemical Changes	https://youtu.be/7Nrma6v0A8I	
5 – Energy Changes	https://youtu.be/PQtjfRolMAE	
6 – The Rate and Extent of Chemical Change	https://youtu.be/C-tHYZwisNs	
7 – Organic Chemistry	https://youtu.be/sE2DP0x48kE	
8 – Chemical Analysis	https://youtu.be/vMKAHdoc-g0	
9 – Chemistry of the Atmosphere	https://youtu.be/DznhhA2QHUg	
10 – Using Resources	https://youtu.be/xBUXqfa2gHo	

Equation Sheet

Percentage yield = $\dfrac{\text{Actual yield}}{\text{Theoretical yield}}$

Atom Economy = $\dfrac{M_r \text{ of atoms in the required products}}{M_r \text{ of reactants}}$

Moles = $\dfrac{\text{mass}}{M_r}$

Concentration (mol/dm^3) = $\dfrac{\text{amount (mol)}}{\text{volume (dm}^3\text{)}}$

Formula of common acids and compounds

Hydrochloric acid	HCl
Sulphuric acid	H_2SO_4
Nitric acid	HNO_3
Water	H_2O
Carbon dioxide	CO_2
Oxygen gas	O_2
Hydrogen gas	H_2
Nitrogen gas	N_2

Reference table of common formulae

They won't give you these in the exam - so learn them!!!

Available as flashcards on my website

As a general rule, elements in group one form +1 ions, group 2 form +2 ions, group 6 form -2 ions and group 7 form -1 ions.

Positive		Negative	
Hydrogen	H^+	Fluoride	F^-
Lithium	Li^+	Chloride	Cl^-
Sodium	Na^+	Bromide	Br^-
Potassium	K^+	Iodide	I^-
Copper (I)	Cu^+	Hydroxide	OH^-
Silver	Ag^+	Nitrate	NO_3^-
Ammonium	NH_4^+	Nitrite	NO_2^-
		Hydrogencarbonate	HCO_3^-
Magnesium	Mg^{2+}	Hydrogensulfate	HSO_4^-
Barium	Ba^{2+}		
Strontium	Sr^{2+}	Sulfate	SO_4^{2-}
Calcium	Ca^{2+}	Carbonate	CO_3^{2-}
Iron (II)	Fe^{2+}	Sulfide	S^{2-}
Copper (II)	Cu^{2+}	Oxide	O^{2-}
Nickel (II)	Ni^{2+}		
Zinc	Zn^{2+}	Nitride	N^{3-}
Tin (II)	Sn^{2+}	Phosphate	PO_4^{3-}
Lead (II)	Pb^{2+}		
Chromium	Cr^{3+}		
Iron (III)	Fe^{3+}		
Aluminium	Al^{3+}		

The Reactivity Series

You need to learn the order and how to use it!

Element	Chemical symbol	Metal or non-metal	How it is found on the earth?	Method of extraction?
Potassium				
Lithium				
Calcium				
Magnesium				
Aluminium				
Carbon				
Zinc				
Iron				
Hydrogen				
Copper				
Silver				
Gold				
Platinum				

Required practical's

1. Making Salts
   - Copper Sulfate Crystals - Separating solids from a solution by filtering and crystallisation   https://youtu.be/ttsAmaNu4ao
   - Practical questions in an exam   https://youtu.be/BmaXoGTAmeA
2. Neutralisation (Chemistry only)
   - How to carry out a titration   https://youtu.be/MDWVrTW0nq8
   - How to read a burette   https://youtu.be/yVF6Gn7HmWk
   - Indicators for titrations - Methyl orange and phenolphthalein
     https://youtu.be/XPTnZnbXgDs
   - Titration Method.   https://youtu.be/2hv2hS6zdh0
3. Electrolysis
   - The electrolysis of sodium sulfate.   https://youtu.be/hcQHxKMpr60
   - The electrolysis of sodium chloride solution (brine).
     https://youtu.be/r0kbEj2PDEg
   - The electrolysis of copper (II) sulfate.   https://youtu.be/L_BjGKdM2Bk
   - The electrolysis of copper (II) chloride.   https://youtu.be/E6npZEyaASk
4. Temperature Changes
   - Temperature change of neutralization.   https://youtu.be/Bz0C9mmF2tw
5. Rates of Reaction
   - Measuring the rate of a reaction by collecting gas - Marble chips and hydrochloric acid   https://youtu.be/SXUWo-V-WgQ
   - Measuring the rate of a reaction by loss of mass
     https://youtu.be/0RUYNpdnALg
   - Measuring the rate of reaction by disappearing cross - Sodium thiosulfate and hydrochloric acid.   https://youtu.be/CwK4-_Xq2yI
6. Chromatography
   - Chromatography.   https://youtu.be/kxrjvLvbY28
   - Chromatography-Why do you need to use a pencil to draw the start line?
     https://youtu.be/4n9LzguhgdQ
7. Ion Identification (Chemistry only)
   - Flame tests for positive ions.   https://youtu.be/i3fEVB9VN0Y
   - Test for Positive Ions.   https://youtu.be/ESQYWh02Ykg
   - Test for Halide Ions.   https://youtu.be/XtQ4hHZzX2k
   - Test for Sulfate Ions.   https://youtu.be/k5qMGgmQDwo
   - Test for Carbonate Ions.   https://youtu.be/7AGBLbl7AHE
   - Anion and Cation Ion Identification Summary (Negative and Positive Ions) and Practice   https://youtu.be/LC4Nxd5dwEM
8. Water purification

Key Words

These are easy marks, but only if you know them!!

Acid	A solution that has a low pH due to the hydrogen ions
Activation energy	The energy needed to start reaction
Alkali	A solution that has a high pH due to hydroxide ions
Alkali metal	Highly reactive metals found on the left-hand side of the periodic table
Alkanes	Hydrocarbon containing only single bonds
Alkenes	Hydrocarbon containing double bonds
Alloy	Mixture of atoms that lead to distorted layers that cannot slide
Atom	Small part of matter, made up from a mixture of protons, neutrons and electrons
Atom economy	A way of determining how many of the reactant atoms made it into the desired product
Atomic number	The number of protons in an atom
Bioleaching	Mining low yield ores using bacteria
Boiling point	Point at which a liquid turns into a gas
Bromine water	Orange liquid that can be used to test for double bonds
Carbon footprint	The atom of carbon that is released into the atmosphere based on your daily activities
Catalyst	Something that speeds up a react of reaction without being use dup
Chromatography	Method of separating out mixtures
Combustion	Burning of a compound in oxygen
Compound	Two or more elements chemically bonded together
Covalent bonding	Sharing of electron between two non-metals
Cracking	Breaking a long hydrocarbon chain to short hydrocarbon chains
Crude oil	A mixture of different length hydrocarbon chains made from decomposing dead plant and animals
Desalination	Removal of salt from water
Diamond	Giant covalent compound where each carbon atom makes four bonds
Displacement	A type of reaction where one element replaces another in a compound
Electrolysis	Separating compounds using electricity
Electron	Found in the shells around the nucleus, has a charge of minus one and no mass
Element	Group of (or single) atoms that all have the same chemical characteristics, can be found on the periodic table
Endothermic	A reaction that takes in energy
Exothermic	A reaction that releases energy
Flammability	The tendency for a substance to catch fire
Formulation	Mixture of compounds

Fractional distillation	Separating out a mixture of different length hydrocarbon chains based upon boiling point
Gas	A state of matter where the atoms move atom in a fast and random matter, can be compressed and flow
Graphite	Giant covalent compound where each carbon atom makes three bonds
Greenhouse gas	Gas that traps infra-red radiation
Halogen	Highly reactive non-metals found on the right-hand side of the periodic table
Hydrocarbon	A compound that only has carbon and hydrogen in it
Ion	Atoms that has lost or gained electrons
Ionic bonding	Transfer of electrons between a metal and a non-metal
Liquid	A state of matter, where the atoms can move and flow but they cannot be compressed
Mass number	the number of protons and neutrons in an atom
Melting point	Point at which a solid turns into a liquid
Metal	On the left-hand side of the periodic table, form positive ions
Mixture	Lots of different elements that may or may not be chemically bonded together
Mole	The molecular mass in grams
Neutralization	Mixing of an acid and an alkali to give a pH of 7
Neutron	Found in the nucleus of atoms, has no charge and a mass of one
Nobel gas	Unreactive gases found on the right of the periodic table
Non-metal	On the right-hand side of the periodic table, form negative ions
Nucleus	In the centre of atoms, contains the protons and the neutrons
Oxidation	Loss of electrons
Percentage yield	A way of determining how much yield you get from a reaction
Periodic table	A way of sorting out the elements
pH	How acid or alkali a solution is
Phytomining	Mining low yield ores using plants
Portable water	Water that is safe to drink
Proton	Found in the nucleus of atoms, has a charge of plus one and a mass of one
Reactivity series	List of metals in order of reactivity
Reduction	Gain of electrons
Reversible reaction	A reaction that can go in either direction
Solid	A state of matter, where the atoms vibrate around a fixed position
Titration	Method for determining concentration of solution
Transition metal	Group of metal that are in the middle of the periodic table, form colour compounds and can be used as catalysts
Viscosity	How easily pourable something is

1 – Atomic Structure and the Periodic Table

Knowledge Checklist

| Specification statement

These are the bits the exam board wants you to know, make sure you can do all of these…	Self-assessment			Bits to help if you don't understand	
	First review 4-7 months before exam	Second review 1-2 months before exam	Final review Week before exam	Primrose Kitten	Other places
I can recall that all substances are made from atoms	☺ 😐 ☹	☺ 😐 ☹	☺ 😐 ☹		TuitionKit http://bit.ly/2h7Gx2F
I can recall the that periodic table shows the range of elements that are known to exist	☺ 😐 ☹	☺ 😐 ☹	☺ 😐 ☹	https://youtu.be/GhOkzDuHIDc	
I can interpret the symbols on the periodic table and use them to identify elements	☺ 😐 ☹	☺ 😐 ☹	☺ 😐 ☹	https://youtu.be/PdujMRxEbn4	
I can define the term compound	☺ 😐 ☹	☺ 😐 ☹	☺ 😐 ☹	https://youtu.be/tguhuiq9tVs	TuitionKit http://bit.ly/2h7Gx2F
I can describe the structure of an atom	☺ 😐 ☹	☺ 😐 ☹	☺ 😐 ☹		TuitionKit http://bit.ly/2h7Gx2F
I can recall the relative size of an atom and a nucleus	☺ 😐 ☹	☺ 😐 ☹	☺ 😐 ☹		
I can recall the relative masses of the three subatomic particles	☺ 😐 ☹	☺ 😐 ☹	☺ 😐 ☹		http://totallearn.co.uk/science-revision/atomicStructure/atomicStructureAdvanced/index.html
I can use the periodic table to state the number of protons, electrons and neutrons in an element	☺ 😐 ☹	☺ 😐 ☹	☺ 😐 ☹	https://youtu.be/ljyzVt8bJSA https://youtu.be/Hq6YMQnROP0	TuitionKit http://bit.ly/2yhbgP4
I can define the terms mass number and atomic number	☺ 😐 ☹	☺ 😐 ☹	☺ 😐 ☹		

Skill				Video	Extra
I can represent a reaction using a word equation	☺😐☹	☺😐☹	☺😐☹	https://youtu.be/X8jiv0qwVok	https://phet.colorado.edu/en/simulation/balancing-chemical-equations
I can represent a reaction using a balanced symbol equation	☺😐☹	☺😐☹	☺😐☹	https://youtu.be/T0wb4z-_kmY https://youtu.be/5GmsOx_DcOM	
I can define the term mixture	☺😐☹	☺😐☹	☺😐☹	https://youtu.be/tguhuiq9tVs	TuitionKit http://bit.ly/2x6vLxn
I can describe different way to separate mixtures using physical processes	☺😐☹	☺😐☹	☺😐☹	https://youtu.be/bAgLzQ_a1jQ	
I can describe how a scientific model can be developed	☺😐☹	☺😐☹	☺😐☹		
I can describe the plum pudding model of the atom	☺😐☹	☺😐☹	☺😐☹	https://youtu.be/nbwcngWsXAU	
I can describe how Rutherford and Marsden's experiments lead to the nuclear model of the atom, and the ideas the Bohr contributed to the model	☺😐☹	☺😐☹	☺😐☹		
I can state the Chadwick showed the existence of the neutrons	☺😐☹	☺😐☹	☺😐☹		
I can draw the electronic structure of the first 20 elements on the periodic table	☺😐☹	☺😐☹	☺😐☹	https://youtu.be/bgWKesHbLnE	TuitionKit http://bit.ly/2w16S54
I can use numbers to represent the electronic structure of the first 20 elements on the periodic table	☺😐☹	☺😐☹	☺😐☹		
I can recall the relative charges of the three subatomic particles	☺😐☹	☺😐☹	☺😐☹		
I can explain why atoms have no overall charge	☺😐☹	☺😐☹	☺😐☹	https://youtu.be/M5qfMT-ePrQ	
I can describe the formation of ions	☺😐☹	☺😐☹	☺😐☹		
I can recall that metals will go on to form positive ions	☺😐☹	☺😐☹	☺😐☹		
I can recall the non-metals will go on to form negative ions	☺😐☹	☺😐☹	☺😐☹		

I can describe the location of metals and non-metals on the periodic table	☺ 😐 ☹	☺ 😐 ☹	☺ 😐 ☹		
I can describe the use of periods and groups to classify parts of the periodic table	☺ 😐 ☹	☺ 😐 ☹	☺ 😐 ☹	https://youtu.be/GhOkzDuHIDc https://youtu.be/8GYMLQt18zQ	
I can describe the development of the early periodic table	☺ 😐 ☹	☺ 😐 ☹	☺ 😐 ☹	https://youtu.be/WXnD0UWlYyk	TuitionKit http://bit.ly/2w0tEtX
I can describe how Mendeleev developed the periodic table	☺ 😐 ☹	☺ 😐 ☹	☺ 😐 ☹		
I can describe the properties of the noble gasses (in group -0)	☺ 😐 ☹	☺ 😐 ☹	☺ 😐 ☹	https://youtu.be/GhOkzDuHIDc	TuitionKit http://bit.ly/2xIH4PM
I can recall that the boiling points of noble gases increase as you go down the periodic table.	☺ 😐 ☹	☺ 😐 ☹	☺ 😐 ☹		
I can describe the properties of group 1 metals	☺ 😐 ☹	☺ 😐 ☹	☺ 😐 ☹	https://youtu.be/UNewX9i1Nh4	TuitionKit http://bit.ly/2h99hEo
I can describe the reactions of group 1 metals	☺ 😐 ☹	☺ 😐 ☹	☺ 😐 ☹	With water; https://youtu.be/t1Kpyyvgncw	
I can recall that the reactivity of group 1 metals increases as you go down the group.	☺ 😐 ☹	☺ 😐 ☹	☺ 😐 ☹	https://youtu.be/5rXKPc-Jy_Y	
I can recall that group 7 element are non-metals and are found as diatomic molecules	☺ 😐 ☹	☺ 😐 ☹	☺ 😐 ☹	https://youtu.be/vK5yc2RR0XQ	TuitionKit http://bit.ly/2fcbxOj
I can describe the reactions of group 7 non-metals	☺ 😐 ☹	☺ 😐 ☹	☺ 😐 ☹		
I can describe the patterns in melting point, boiling point and reactivity in group 7	☺ 😐 ☹	☺ 😐 ☹	☺ 😐 ☹		
I can describe displacement reaction in relation to group 7 elements	☺ 😐 ☹	☺ 😐 ☹	☺ 😐 ☹		
I can describe the properties of transition metals **Chemistry only**	☺ 😐 ☹	☺ 😐 ☹	☺ 😐 ☹	https://youtu.be/Tw3NJ_it3tc	TuitionKit http://bit.ly/2h7pk9G
I can describe the uses of transition metals **Chemistry only**	☺ 😐 ☹	☺ 😐 ☹	☺ 😐 ☹		

| I can recall that transition metals form different coloured compounds **Chemistry only** | ☺ ☻ ☹ | ☺ ☻ ☹ | ☺ ☻ ☹ | | |

Quick fire questions;

This worksheet is fully supported by a video tutorial; https://youtu.be/mjlIPJ_c018

1. What element is represented by W?
2. What element is represented by Na?
3. What element is represented by Si?
4. What element is represented by Co?
5. What element is represented by Fe?
6. What group is oxygen in?
7. What group is argon in?
8. What group is potassium in?
9. What group is sulfur in?
10. What group is chlorine in?
11. What period is phosphorous in?
12. What period is nitrogen in?
13. What period is calcium in?
14. What period is gallium in?
15. What period is carbon in?
16. What is a compound?
17. What is a mixture?
18. Give three ways of separating out mixtures.
19. What is the name for CO_2?
20. What is the name for H_2O?
21. What did Chadwick discover?
22. What experiment did Rutherford do?
23. What type of foil did Rutherford use?
24. What did Rutherford fire at the foil?
25. What model of the atom was Rutherford testing?
26. What did Rutherford discover?
27. What was the new model of the atom called?
28. Where are electrons?
29. Where are protons?
30. Where are neutrons?
31. What charge do protons have?
32. What charge do neutrons have?
33. What charge do electrons have?
34. What mass do protons have?

35. What mass do electrons have?
36. What mass do neutrons have?
37. What does the atomic number tell us?
38. What does the mass number tell us?
39. How do you find the number of protons in an atom?
40. How do you find the number of electrons in an atom?
41. How do you find the number of neutrons in an atom?
42. How do you find the number of protons in an ion?
43. How do you find the number of electrons in an ion?
44. How do you find the number of neutrons in an ion?
45. How many electrons fit on the first shell?
46. How many electrons fit on the second shell?
47. How many electrons fit on the third shell?
48. What element has the electronic structure 2,8,1?
49. What element has the electronic structure 2,3?
50. What element has the electronic structure 2,8,5?
51. What element has the electronic structure 2?
52. What element has the electronic structure 2,8,8,1?
53. What type of ions do metals form (positive/negative)?
54. What type of ions do non-metals form (positive/negative)?
55. What bonding occurs between two non-metals?
56. What bonding occurs between a metal and a non-metal?
57. What happens to the electrons in covalent bonding?
58. What happens to the electrons in ionic bonding?
59. How did Mendeleev organise his periodic table?
60. Why did Mendeleev leave gaps in his periodic table?
61. On which side (left/right) of the periodic table are metals found?
62. On which side (left/right) of the periodic table are non-metals found?
63. What is another name for group 1?
64. How reactive are group 1 elements?
65. How does reactivity change as you go down group 1?
66. How does sodium react with water?
67. How does sodium react with oxygen?
68. How does sodium react with chlorine?
69. What is another name for group 0/8?
70. How reactive are group 0 elements?
71. How does boiling point change as you go down group 0?
72. What is another name for group 7?

73. How reactive are group 7 elements?
74. How does boiling point change as you go down group 7?
75. How does reactivity change as you go down group 7?

GCSE Chemistry Separate Science Only

76. What are the properties of transition metals?
77. Give a use for transition metals
78. What colour does iron (II) go?
79. What colour does iron (III) go?
80. What colour does copper (II) go?

2 – Bonding, Structure and the Properties of Matter

Knowledge Checklist

| Specification statement

These are the bits the exam board wants you to know, make sure you can do all of these...	Self-assessment			Bits to help if you don't understand	
	First review 4-7 months before exam	Second review 1-2 months before exam	Final review Week before exam	Primrose Kitten	Other places
I can represent a solid, a liquid and a gas by drawing the arrangement of atoms	☺😐☹	☺😐☹	☺😐☹	https://youtu.be/hs9DIOqzgRg	TuitionKit http://bit.ly/2h9Yfma
I can recall that energy is needed to change state	☺😐☹	☺😐☹	☺😐☹		
I can predict the state of a substance at a given temperature	☺😐☹	☺😐☹	☺😐☹		
I can use appropriate state symbol in an equation	☺😐☹	☺😐☹	☺😐☹		
I can recall that ionic bonding occurs between a metal and a non-metal	☺😐☹	☺😐☹	☺😐☹	https://youtu.be/TI6xRyWDtok	TuitionKit http://bit.ly/2xqBlNt
I can describe the formation of ions	☺😐☹	☺😐☹	☺😐☹	https://youtu.be/M5qfMT-ePrQ	http://bit.ly/2x5Jo2A
I can recall that metals will go on to form positive ions	☺😐☹	☺😐☹	☺😐☹	https://youtu.be/746sTyJqrJo	
I can recall the non-metals will go on to form negative ions	☺😐☹	☺😐☹	☺😐☹	https://youtu.be/9K3RvTq-LwU	
I can describe the location of metals and non-metals on the periodic table	☺😐☹	☺😐☹	☺😐☹		
I can describe ionic bonding as the strong electrostatic attraction between oppositely charged ions	☺😐☹	☺😐☹	☺😐☹		
I can draw dot and cross diagrams to show ionic bonding between group 1 and group 2 metals and group 6 and group 7 non-metals.	☺😐☹	☺😐☹	☺😐☹	https://youtu.be/gbx1pcFn4ws	

Primrose Kitten – YouTube Tutorials for Science and Maths.

Skill				Link	Link
I can recall that covalent bonding occurs between 2 non-metals	☺😐☹	☺😐☹	☺😐☹	https://youtu.be/4I4IqZ2qcfU	TuitionKit http://bit.ly/2h8thL0 http://bit.ly/2xID3e0
I can represent the bonding in covalent compounds as a dot and cross diagram (hydrogen, chlorine, oxygen, nitrogen, hydrogen chloride, ammonia and methane)	☺😐☹	☺😐☹	☺😐☹		
I can draw covalent compounds using lines to represent electron pairs	☺😐☹	☺😐☹	☺😐☹		
I can recall the names and formula of common covalent compounds	☺😐☹	☺😐☹	☺😐☹		
I can recall that covalent compounds can be small and simple or giant.	☺😐☹	☺😐☹	☺😐☹		
I can work out the formula of a compound from a picture	☺😐☹	☺😐☹	☺😐☹		
I can explain how strong metallic bonds arise	☺😐☹	☺😐☹	☺😐☹		TuitionKit http://bit.ly/2x7YzG2
I can explain why most metal have high melting and boiling points	☺😐☹	☺😐☹	☺😐☹		
I can describe the pattern of atoms in a pure metal	☺😐☹	☺😐☹	☺😐☹		
I can explain why pure metals are not used often	☺😐☹	☺😐☹	☺😐☹		
I can describe and explain the arrangement of atoms in an alloy	☺😐☹	☺😐☹	☺😐☹		
I can describe the advantages of an alloy over pure metals	☺😐☹	☺😐☹	☺😐☹	https://youtu.be/Lgfskmrx3Aw	TuitionKit http://bit.ly/2xcaxQJ
I can explain how metals conduct electricity	☺😐☹	☺😐☹	☺😐☹		
I can describe the structure of an ionic compounds	☺😐☹	☺😐☹	☺😐☹	https://youtu.be/TI6xRyWDtok	http://totallearn.co.uk/science-revision/calculations/molecularFormula/index.html
I can describe the properties of an ionic compounds	☺😐☹	☺😐☹	☺😐☹		
I can describe the structure of a simple covalent compounds	☺😐☹	☺😐☹	☺😐☹		http://totallearn.co.uk/science-revision/bond
I can describe the properties of a simple covalent compounds	☺😐☹	☺😐☹	☺😐☹		

I can describe the structure of a giant covalent compounds	☺ ☹ ☹	☺ ☹ ☹	☺ ☹ ☹		ing/bondingCovalent/index.html
I can describe the properties of a giant covalent compounds	☺ ☹ ☹	☺ ☹ ☹	☺ ☹ ☹		
I can use experimental data to determine if a compound is ionic, simple covalent or giant covalent.	☺ ☹ ☹	☺ ☹ ☹	☺ ☹ ☹		
I can describe the structure of a polymer	☺ ☹ ☹	☺ ☹ ☹	☺ ☹ ☹		TuitionKit http://bit.ly/2xIoIyo
I can describe the properties of a polymer	☺ ☹ ☹	☺ ☹ ☹	☺ ☹ ☹		
I can describe how the bonding in diamond affects the properties	☺ ☹ ☹	☺ ☹ ☹	☺ ☹ ☹		
I can explain the difference in bonding between diamond and graphite	☺ ☹ ☹	☺ ☹ ☹	☺ ☹ ☹		
I can describe how the bonding in graphite affects the properties	☺ ☹ ☹	☺ ☹ ☹	☺ ☹ ☹		
I can describe how the structure of graphene give it properties that can be useful in the modern world	☺ ☹ ☹	☺ ☹ ☹	☺ ☹ ☹		TuitionKit http://bit.ly/2frJuHO
I can describe how the structure of fullerenes give them properties that can be useful in the modern world	☺ ☹ ☹	☺ ☹ ☹	☺ ☹ ☹		
I can describe how the structure of carbon nanotubes give them properties that can be useful in the modern world	☺ ☹ ☹	☺ ☹ ☹	☺ ☹ ☹		
I can recall the size of nanoparticles **Chemistry only**	☺ ☹ ☹	☺ ☹ ☹	☺ ☹ ☹		TuitionKit http://bit.ly/2fdhk6c
I can recall why nanoparticle have different properties **Chemistry only**	☺ ☹ ☹	☺ ☹ ☹	☺ ☹ ☹		The strange new world of Nanoscience, narrated by Stephen Fry http://bit.ly/2wseIVH
I can describe the uses of nanoparticles **Chemistry only**	☺ ☹ ☹	☺ ☹ ☹	☺ ☹ ☹		
I can discuss the advantages and disadvantage of using nanoparticles **Chemistry only**	☺ ☹ ☹	☺ ☹ ☹	☺ ☹ ☹		

Quick fire questions;

This worksheet is fully supported by a video tutorial; https://youtu.be/9bbCFUyluWg

1. Draw the arrangement of particles in a solid.
2. Draw the arrangement of particles in a liquid.
3. Draw the arrangement of particles in a gas.
4. What is it called when a solid turns into liquid?
5. What is it called when a liquid turns into a gas?
6. What is it called when a gas turns into liquid?
7. What is it called when a liquid turns into a solid?
8. What is the boiling point?
9. What is the condensing point?
10. What does this state symbol mean (s)?
11. What does this state symbol mean (l)?
12. What does this state symbol mean (g)?
13. What does this state symbol mean (aq)?
14. What is ionic bonding?
15. How are ions formed?
16. What type of ions with a metal form?
17. What type of ions will a non-metal form?
18. Where are metals on the periodic table
19. Where are non-metals on the periodic table?
20. What is an ionic bond?
21. Draw a dot and cross diagram to show the bonding in sodium chloride.
22. Draw a dot and cross diagram to show the bonding in magnesium chloride.
23. Draw a dot and cross diagram to show the bonding in magnesium oxide.
24. What is covalent bonding?
25. List six simple covalent compounds.
26. Give the formula of oxygen gas.
27. Give the formula of nitrogen gas.
28. Give the formula of hydrogen chloride.
29. Give the formula of ammonia.
30. Give the formula of methane.
31. Give the formula of hydrogen gas.
32. Give the formula of water.
33. Give the formula of carbon dioxide.
34. Draw the bonding in water.

35. Draw the bonding in carbon dioxide.
36. Draw the bonding in chlorine gas.
37. Draw the bonding in nitrogen gas.
38. Draw the bonding in oxygen gas.
39. Draw the bonding in hydrochloric acid.
40. Draw the bonding in ammonia.
41. Draw the bonding in methane.
42. In a covalent bonding diagram what does each line represent?
43. Give two examples of giant covalent compounds.
44. How does metallic bonding arise?
45. Why do metals have high boiling and melting points?
46. How are atoms in a pure metal arranged?
47. How are atoms in an alloy arranged?
48. Why do people use alloys and not pure metals?
49. How do metals conduct electricity?
50. Describe the structure of an ionic compound.
51. Describe the properties of an ionic compound.
52. Describe the structure of a simple covalent compound.
53. Describe the properties of a simple covalent compound.
54. Describe the structure of giant covalent compound.
55. Describe the properties of a giant covalent compound.
56. What is a monomer?
57. What is a polymer?
58. Describe the structure of a polymer.
59. Which element is both diamond and graphite made from?
60. Describe the bonding in diamond.
61. Describe the difference between the bonding in diamonds and the bonding in graphite?
62. What are the properties of graphite?
63. What are the uses of graphene?
64. What are the uses of fullerenes?
65. Describe the structure of fullerenes.
66. Describe the structure of carbon nanotubes.

Chemistry only

67. What is the size of a nanoparticle?
68. Why do nanoparticles have different properties?
69. What can nanoparticle be used for?
70. What are the advantages and disadvantages of nanoparticles?

3 – Quantitative Chemistry

Knowledge Checklist

Specification statement These are the bits the exam board wants you to know, make sure you can do all of these…	Self-assessment			Bits to help if you don't understand	
	First review 4-7 months before exam	Second review 1-2 months before exam	Final review Week before exam	Primrose Kitten	Other places
I can describe different ways of measuring the mass or volume of a product of a reactant	☺ 😐 ☹	☺ 😐 ☹	☺ 😐 ☹		
I can explain why the mass of a reaction appears to change	☺ 😐 ☹	☺ 😐 ☹	☺ 😐 ☹	https://youtu.be/WqhZBnR743I	
I can explain that in any measurement there is a degree of uncertainty	☺ 😐 ☹	☺ 😐 ☹	☺ 😐 ☹		
I can calculate the concentration of a solution from the masses used	☺ 😐 ☹	☺ 😐 ☹	☺ 😐 ☹		
I can represent a reaction using a word equation	☺ 😐 ☹	☺ 😐 ☹	☺ 😐 ☹	https://youtu.be/X8jiv0qwVok	
I can represent a reaction using a balanced symbol equation	☺ 😐 ☹	☺ 😐 ☹	☺ 😐 ☹	https://youtu.be/T0wb4z-_kmY https://youtu.be/5GmsOx_DcOM	TuitionKit http://bit.ly/2ymP1Hf
I can calculate the relative formula mass (M_r) of a compound from the relative atomic (A_r) masses of the elements	☺ 😐 ☹	☺ 😐 ☹	☺ 😐 ☹	https://youtu.be/8W9D8fiNodQ https://youtu.be/EPX7UKE22Gs	TuitionKit http://bit.ly/2jHbk7h Total Learn http://bit.ly/2xk1MUD
I can define the term mole **Higher tier only**	☺ 😐 ☹	☺ 😐 ☹	☺ 😐 ☹		
I can calculate the number of moles from the mass **Higher tier only**	☺ 😐 ☹	☺ 😐 ☹	☺ 😐 ☹	https://youtu.be/JN_qmij-pkQ	TuitionKit http://bit.ly/2xNfoJt

I can describe the number of particles in one mole as being equal to Avogadro's constant **Higher tier only**	☺ 😐 ☹	☺ 😐 ☹	☺ 😐 ☹		
I can calculate the mass of a reactant or a product given the equation **Higher tier only**	☺ 😐 ☹	☺ 😐 ☹	☺ 😐 ☹		TuitionKit http://bit.ly/2hdquAp
I can balance equation given information about the number of moles involved. **Higher tier only**	☺ 😐 ☹	☺ 😐 ☹	☺ 😐 ☹		
I can describe when a reactant would be used in excess **Higher tier only**	☺ 😐 ☹	☺ 😐 ☹	☺ 😐 ☹		
I can calculate the percentage yield of a reaction **Chemistry only**	☺ 😐 ☹	☺ 😐 ☹	☺ 😐 ☹		TuitionKit http://bit.ly/2w5C17y
I can calculate the atom economy of a reaction **Chemistry only**	☺ 😐 ☹	☺ 😐 ☹	☺ 😐 ☹		TuitionKit http://bit.ly/2hfcVgn
I can explain why a reaction may not give the expected yield **Chemistry only**	☺ 😐 ☹	☺ 😐 ☹	☺ 😐 ☹		TuitionKit http://bit.ly/2fi3xLG
I can carry out a titration	☺ 😐 ☹	☺ 😐 ☹	☺ 😐 ☹	https://youtu.be/MDWVrTW0ng8 https://youtu.be/yVF6Gn7HmWk https://youtu.be/XPTnZnbXgDs https://youtu.be/2hv2hS6zdh0	
I can calculate the concentration of a solution in mol/dm^3 **Chemistry only** **Higher tier only**	☺ 😐 ☹	☺ 😐 ☹	☺ 😐 ☹	https://youtu.be/hhkt3ZZ-pvQ	TuitionKit http://bit.ly/2hctzk5
I can carry out titration calculations **Chemistry only** **Higher tier only**	☺ 😐 ☹	☺ 😐 ☹	☺ 😐 ☹		

I can recall that a gas takes up 24dm^3 under standard condition **Chemistry only** **Higher tier only**	☺ 😐 ☹	☺ 😐 ☹	☺ 😐 ☹		
I can calculate the volume of a gas **Chemistry only** **Higher tier only**	☺ 😐 ☹	☺ 😐 ☹	☺ 😐 ☹		TuitionKit http://bit.ly/2yoA3ka

Quick fire questions;

This worksheet is fully supported by a video tutorial; https://youtu.be/8uqWdmIKd7c

1. Give three ways of measuring the mass or volume of a product or a reactant.
2. How do you calculate the concentration of a solution?
3. Give the formula of oxygen gas.
4. Give the formula of nitrogen gas.
5. Give the formula of hydrogen chloride.
6. Give the formula of ammonia.
7. Give the formula of methane.
8. Give the formula of hydrogen gas.
9. Give the formula of water.
10. Give the formula of carbon dioxide.
11. Balance this N_2 +..........H_2 → ....NH_3
12. Balance this $CaCl_2$ + KOH → $Ca(OH)_2$ + KCl
13. Ammonia reacts with oxygen gas; write this as a balanced symbol equation.
14. Magnesium reacts with carbon dioxide; write this is a balanced symbol equation.
15. Define relative formula mass (M_r).
16. Define relative atomic mass (A_r).
17. What is the mass of argon?
18. What is the mass of calcium?
19. What is the mass of H_2SO_4?
20. What is the mass of MgO?

Higher tier only

21. What does the term mole mean?
22. What is equation for calculating moles?
23. What is Avogadro's constant?

Chemistry only

24. How do you calculate percentage yield of reaction?
25. How do you calculate the atom economy of a reaction?
26. Why might a reaction not give the expected yield?
27. What is the colour change in phenolphthalein?
28. What is the colour change in the methyl orange?

Higher tier

29. How do you calculate the concentration of the solution?
30. How much volume does 1 moles of gas take up at standard conditions?

The content of this topic (and a few earlier bits) are covered in my book; Maths (The Chemistry Bits) for Science Students. Available from my website or Amazon

- Periodic Table
- Mass number and atomic number
- The number of protons, neutrons and electrons
- Isotopes
- Ions
- Elements and atoms
- Brackets
- Conservation of mass
- Balancing equations
- Relative formula mass
- Calculating relative atomic mass or relative isotopic mass
- Moles
- Percentage yield
- Atom economy
- Half equations
- Reacting masses
- Avogadro's constant and gas volume
- Endothermic and exothermic reactions
- Bond energy questions
- Titration calculations

4 – Chemical Changes

Knowledge Checklist

| Specification statement

These are the bits the exam board wants you to know, make sure you can do all of these…	Self-assessment			Bits to help if you don't understand	
	First review 4-7 months before exam	Second review 1-2 months before exam	Final review Week before exam	Primrose Kitten	Other places
I can describe the reaction between metal and oxygen	☺ 😐 ☹	☺ 😐 ☹	☺ 😐 ☹		
I can recall the order of the reactivity series	☺ 😐 ☹	☺ 😐 ☹	☺ 😐 ☹		TuitionKit http://bit.ly/2xv1LNZ
I can describe when a displacement reaction might take place	☺ 😐 ☹	☺ 😐 ☹	☺ 😐 ☹	https://youtu.be/7Pm5-ox6YGM	
I can use experimental data to work out the order of reactivity	☺ 😐 ☹	☺ 😐 ☹	☺ 😐 ☹		
I can describe how unreactive metals are found in the Earth	☺ 😐 ☹	☺ 😐 ☹	☺ 😐 ☹		
I can describe reduction	☺ 😐 ☹	☺ 😐 ☹	☺ 😐 ☹		
I can describe the process of extracting aluminium by electrolysis	☺ 😐 ☹	☺ 😐 ☹	☺ 😐 ☹		TuitionKit http://bit.ly/2heSYpD
I can describe oxidation as the loss of electrons
Higher tier only	☺ 😐 ☹	☺ 😐 ☹	☺ 😐 ☹	"OILRIG" https://youtu.be/-5fL5IOPSfs	
I can describe reduction as a gain of electrons
Higher tier only	☺ 😐 ☹	☺ 😐 ☹	☺ 😐 ☹		
I can write balanced ionic half equations
Higher tier only	☺ 😐 ☹	☺ 😐 ☹	☺ 😐 ☹	https://youtu.be/vbic3491cE8	
I can determine which element in a reaction is oxidised or reduced from the equation
Higher tier only	☺ 😐 ☹	☺ 😐 ☹	☺ 😐 ☹		

Skill				Video	Other
I can use the general equation to give the products from a reaction	☺ 😐 ☹	☺ 😐 ☹	☺ 😐 ☹	https://youtu.be/Sh3tOH95-AQ https://youtu.be/Gstk2bhzBVQ https://youtu.be/-kwhGkvUjoQ	TuitionKit http://bit.ly/2hdd7QE Total Learn http://bit.ly/2w4JYJZ
I can determine the formula of a salt from common ions	☺ 😐 ☹	☺ 😐 ☹	☺ 😐 ☹		Common ions flash cards on www.primrosekitten.com
I can describe how to make a pure salt	☺ 😐 ☹	☺ 😐 ☹	☺ 😐 ☹	RP1; https://youtu.be/ttsAmaNu4ao https://youtu.be/BmaXoGTAmeA	TuitionKit http://bit.ly/2yoMoF8
I can describe the ions that lead to acidic and alkaline conditions	☺ 😐 ☹	☺ 😐 ☹	☺ 😐 ☹	https://youtu.be/CvmhbNYroeo	
I can use the pH scale to describe how acidic or alkaline a solution is	☺ 😐 ☹	☺ 😐 ☹	☺ 😐 ☹		TuitionKit http://bit.ly/2xkyZzj
I can use an equation to show neutralisation	☺ 😐 ☹	☺ 😐 ☹	☺ 😐 ☹		
I can carry out a titration	☺ 😐 ☹	☺ 😐 ☹	☺ 😐 ☹	https://youtu.be/MDWVrTW0nq8 https://youtu.be/yVF6Gn7HmWk https://youtu.be/XPTnZnbXgDs https://youtu.be/2hv2hS6zdh0	TuitionKit http://bit.ly/2xOvRgx
I can calculate a concentration from titration data **Chemistry only**	☺ 😐 ☹	☺ 😐 ☹	☺ 😐 ☹	https://youtu.be/hhkt3ZZ-pvQ	
I can give examples of strong and weak acids **Higher tier only**	☺ 😐 ☹	☺ 😐 ☹	☺ 😐 ☹	https://youtu.be/bdUas8qRUew	TuitionKit http://bit.ly/2f7RL2N

I can describe how concentration relates to pH **Higher tier only**	☺ ☹ ☹	☺ ☹ ☹	☺ ☹ ☹		Total Learn http://bit.ly/2fg1gAL
I can use the terms strong, weak, concentrated and dilute in term of acids **Higher tier only**	☺ ☹ ☹	☺ ☹ ☹	☺ ☹ ☹		
I can explain why compounds need to be molten or dissolved to conduct	☺ ☹ ☹	☺ ☹ ☹	☺ ☹ ☹		
I can describe the movement of ions during electrolysis	☺ ☹ ☹	☺ ☹ ☹	☺ ☹ ☹	https://youtu.be/m1NURA22XTk	
I can predict the products of electrolysis	☺ ☹ ☹	☺ ☹ ☹	☺ ☹ ☹	RP5; https://youtu.be/hcQHxKMpr60 https://youtu.be/xCSa3YQbGRc https://youtu.be/r0kbEj2PDEg https://youtu.be/L_BjGKdM2Bk https://youtu.be/E6npZEyaASk	TuitionKit http://bit.ly/2xudbBI
I can write balanced half equations to describe what happens at each electrode	☺ ☹ ☹	☺ ☹ ☹	☺ ☹ ☹	https://youtu.be/vbic3491cE8	TuitionKit http://bit.ly/2xbbnOe
I can describe how to test for the production of chlorine gas	☺ ☹ ☹	☺ ☹ ☹	☺ ☹ ☹		
I can describe how to test for the production of hydrogen gas	☺ ☹ ☹	☺ ☹ ☹	☺ ☹ ☹	https://youtu.be/wuNB1n5z9QM	
I can describe how to test for the production of oxygen gas	☺ ☹ ☹	☺ ☹ ☹	☺ ☹ ☹		
I can describe what happens to aqueous solutions that are electrolysed	☺ ☹ ☹	☺ ☹ ☹	☺ ☹ ☹		

Quick fire questions;

This worksheet is fully supported by a video tutorial; https://youtu.be/7Nrma6v0A8I

1. Describe what happens when a metal reacts with oxygen.
2. List the order of the reactivity series.
3. How are unreactive metals found?
4. What is the formula of magnesium oxide?
5. What is the formula of calcium hydroxide?
6. What ion is responsible for acidity?
7. What ion is responsible for alkalinity?
8. Is pH1 acid, alkali or neutral?
9. Is pH7 acid, alkali or neutral?
10. Is pH14 acid, alkali or neutral?
11. Write down the neutralisation equation.
12. When do ionic compounds conduct electricity?
13. Why do ionic compounds need to molten or dissolved to conduct?
14. What happens to positive ions during electrolysis?
15. What happens negative ions during electrolysis?
16. If a metal chloride is being electrolysed what gas will be produced?
17. If metal sulfate is being electrolysed what gas will be produced?
18. How do you test for chlorine gas?
19. How do you test for hydrogen gas?
20. How do you test for oxygen gas?

Higher tier only

21. What is reduction?
22. What is oxidation?
23. Balance this ....Cl^- .... $\rightarrow Cl_2$
24. Balance this Mg^{2+} .... $\rightarrow Mg$
25. Give an example of a strong acid.
26. Give an example of a weak acid.
27. What is a concentrated acid?
28. What is a dilute acid?

5 – Energy Changes

Knowledge Checklist

Specification statement These are the bits the exam board wants you to know, make sure you can do all of these…	Self-assessment			Bits to help if you don't understand	
	First review 4-7 months before exam	Second review 1-2 months before exam	Final review Week before exam	Primrose Kitten	Other places
I can describe the energy changes in an exothermic or and endothermic reaction	☺ 😐 ☹	☺ 😐 ☹	☺ 😐 ☹	RP4; https://youtu.be/ Bz0C9mmF2tw	TuitionKit http://bit.ly /2xe67a7
I can give uses for endothermic and exothermic reactions	☺ 😐 ☹	☺ 😐 ☹	☺ 😐 ☹		
I can draw the reaction profiles for endothermic and exothermic reactions	☺ 😐 ☹	☺ 😐 ☹	☺ 😐 ☹	https://youtu.be/ bMndHV8m-w8	TuitionKit http://bit.ly /2ybyoxk
I can determine the energy change in a reaction	☺ 😐 ☹	☺ 😐 ☹	☺ 😐 ☹	https://youtu.be/ kvxTE-U-oZY	TuitionKit http://bit.ly /2xjL8ob
I can recall that energy is needed to break bonds **Higher tier only**	☺ 😐 ☹	☺ 😐 ☹	☺ 😐 ☹	https://youtu.be/ 0HxSWa_36_s	
I can recall that energy is released when bonds are made **Higher tier only**	☺ 😐 ☹	☺ 😐 ☹	☺ 😐 ☹		
I can calculate the energy change in a reaction **Higher tier only**	☺ 😐 ☹	☺ 😐 ☹	☺ 😐 ☹	https://youtu.be/ B3hs4GEgJQc	
I can describe how a simple cell works **Chemistry only**	☺ 😐 ☹	☺ 😐 ☹	☺ 😐 ☹		TuitionKit http://bit.ly /2f81p5A
I can recall that a battery is two or more cells **Chemistry only**	☺ 😐 ☹	☺ 😐 ☹	☺ 😐 ☹		

I can describe the difference between rechargeable and non-rechargeable batteries **Chemistry only**	☺ ☹ ☹	☺ ☹ ☹	☺ ☹ ☹		
I can describe the reaction in a hydrogen fuel cell **Chemistry only**	☺ ☹ ☹	☺ ☹ ☹	☺ ☹ ☹	https://youtu.be/sO4uUdKpDEo	TuitionKit http://bit.ly/2w51Gx2
I can evaluate the use of hydrogen fuel cells **Chemistry only**	☺ ☹ ☹	☺ ☹ ☹	☺ ☹ ☹		
I can write half equations for the reactions that take place **Chemistry only**	☺ ☹ ☹	☺ ☹ ☹	☺ ☹ ☹		

Quick fire questions;

This worksheet is fully supported by a video tutorial; https://youtu.be/PQtjfRolMAE

1. Define exothermic.
2. Define endothermic.
3. Draw the reaction profile for an endothermic reaction.
4. Draw the reaction profile for an exothermic reaction.
5. If energy is needed what is happening to the bonds?
6. If energy is released what is happening to the bonds?
7. How do you calculate the energy change in a reaction?

Chemistry only

8. How does simple cell work?
9. What is the difference between a battery and cell?
10. What is the difference between rechargeable non-rechargeable batteries?

6 – The Rate and Extent of Chemical Change

Knowledge Checklist

Specification statement These are the bits the exam board wants you to know, make sure you can do all of these…	Self-assessment			Bits to help if you don't understand	
	First review 4-7 months before exam	Second review 1-2 months before exam	Final review Week before exam	Primrose Kitten	Other places
I can calculate the mean rate of a reaction	☺ 😐 ☹	☺ 😐 ☹	☺ 😐 ☹		TuitionKit http://bit.ly /2xO6go6
I can recall ways to measure the quantity of a reactant of product	☺ 😐 ☹	☺ 😐 ☹	☺ 😐 ☹		
I can recall the units for measuring rate of reaction	☺ 😐 ☹	☺ 😐 ☹	☺ 😐 ☹		
I can give the quantity of a reactant in moles	☺ 😐 ☹	☺ 😐 ☹	☺ 😐 ☹		
I can draw a graph to show the progress of a reaction by showing the reactant being used up or a product being formed	☺ 😐 ☹	☺ 😐 ☹	☺ 😐 ☹		
I can draw tangents to curves and interpret the slope of these	☺ 😐 ☹	☺ 😐 ☹	☺ 😐 ☹		
I can calculate the gradient of a curve from the tangent	☺ 😐 ☹	☺ 😐 ☹	☺ 😐 ☹		
I can describe how to investigate the rate of a reaction	☺ 😐 ☹	☺ 😐 ☹	☺ 😐 ☹	RP; https://youtu.be/ SXUWo-V-WgQ https://youtu.be/ 0RUYNpdnALg https://youtu.be/ CwK4-_Xq2yI	
I can describe and explain how a change in temperature will affect a rate of a reaction	☺ 😐 ☹	☺ 😐 ☹	☺ 😐 ☹		TuitionKit http://bit.ly /2xP6lrA

I can describe and explain how a change in pressure will affect a rate of a reaction	☺ 😐 ☹	☺ 😐 ☹	☺ 😐 ☹		
I can describe and explain how a change in concentration will affect a rate of a reaction	☺ 😐 ☹	☺ 😐 ☹	☺ 😐 ☹		
I can describe and explain how a change in surface area will affect a rate of a reaction	☺ 😐 ☹	☺ 😐 ☹	☺ 😐 ☹	https://youtu.be/IdVJpLQEFKw https://youtu.be/IdVJpLQEFKw	
I can describe and explain how catalyst will affect a rate of a reaction	☺ 😐 ☹	☺ 😐 ☹	☺ 😐 ☹		
I can use collision theory to explain how different factors (temperature/ pressure/ concentration/ surface area) will affect the rate of a reaction	☺ 😐 ☹	☺ 😐 ☹	☺ 😐 ☹		
I can describe how a catalyst lowers activation energy	☺ 😐 ☹	☺ 😐 ☹	☺ 😐 ☹		
I can draw an energy profile diagram for a catalysed and an uncatalysed reaction	☺ 😐 ☹	☺ 😐 ☹	☺ 😐 ☹		
I can use symbols to represent a reversible reaction	☺ 😐 ☹	☺ 😐 ☹	☺ 😐 ☹		TuitionKit http://bit.ly/2hcggjQ
I can describe what happens to ammonium chloride upon heating and cooling	☺ 😐 ☹	☺ 😐 ☹	☺ 😐 ☹		
I can describe what happens to copper sulfate upon addition and removal of water	☺ 😐 ☹	☺ 😐 ☹	☺ 😐 ☹	https://youtu.be/Ie2P68YfYWIv	
I can describe what happens to the energy in a reversible reaction, where one direction is exothermic and the other is endothermic **Higher tier only**	☺ 😐 ☹	☺ 😐 ☹	☺ 😐 ☹		TuitionKit http://bit.ly/2f6YNEY
I can describe what is happening to the rate of reactions when they have reached equilibrium **Higher tier only**	☺ 😐 ☹	☺ 😐 ☹	☺ 😐 ☹		TuitionKit http://bit.ly/2yaWloC

I can determine the effects that a change in temperature will have on the system, according to Le Chatelier's Principle **Higher tier only**	☺ 😐 ☹	☺ 😐 ☹	☺ 😐 ☹		TuitionKit http://bit.ly/2ynjLb5
I can determine the effects that a change in concentration will have on the system, according to Le Chatelier's Principle **Higher tier only**	☺ 😐 ☹	☺ 😐 ☹	☺ 😐 ☹		
I can determine the effects that a change in pressure will have on the system, according to Le Chatelier's Principle **Higher tier only**	☺ 😐 ☹	☺ 😐 ☹	☺ 😐 ☹		TuitionKit http://bit.ly/2fiboJb

Quick fire questions

This worksheet is fully supported by a video tutorial; https://youtu.be/C-tHYZwisNs

1. How do you measure the rate of reaction?
2. Give two ways to measure the quantity of reactant or product.
3. What are the units for measuring rate of reaction?
4. How do you calculate the gradient for a tangent?
5. Give three ways to measure the rate of reaction.
6. How can a change in temperature affect the rate of reaction?
7. How a change in pressure affect the rate of reaction?
8. How can a change in concentration affect the rate of reaction?
9. How can a change in surface area affect the rate of reaction?
10. What is a catalyst?
11. How can a catalyst affect the rate of reaction?
12. Sketch an energy profile for catalysed and an uncatalysed reaction.
13. What symbol represents a reversible reaction?
14. What happens to ammonium chloride upon heating and cooling?
15. What happens to copper sulfate on the addition and removal of water?

Higher tier only

16. What is Le Chatelier's Principle

7 – Organic Chemistry

Knowledge Checklist

Specification statement These are the bits the exam board wants you to know, make sure you can do all of these…	Self-assessment			Bits to help if you don't understand	
	First review 4-7 months before exam	Second review 1-2 months before exam	Final review Week before exam	Primrose Kitten	Other places
I can define the term hydrocarbon	☺ 😐 ☹	☺ 😐 ☹	☺ 😐 ☹	https://youtu.be/ VdstfH3CbvU https://youtu.be/ FE_wFJDXm8E	TuitionKit http://bit.ly /2hgdYww
I can describe the makeup of crude oil	☺ 😐 ☹	☺ 😐 ☹	☺ 😐 ☹	https://youtu.be/ XXncE3cZ4H8	
I can give and use the general formula for alkanes	☺ 😐 ☹	☺ 😐 ☹	☺ 😐 ☹	https://youtu.be/ 5kpo5W0UaX8	
I can name and draw the first 4 alkanes	☺ 😐 ☹	☺ 😐 ☹	☺ 😐 ☹		
I can recall why we need to distil oil into fractions	☺ 😐 ☹	☺ 😐 ☹	☺ 😐 ☹	https://youtu.be/ XXncE3cZ4H8 https://youtu.be/ eUmRR7y5HGc	
I can state some uses for the fractions of crude oil	☺ 😐 ☹	☺ 😐 ☹	☺ 😐 ☹		
I can describe the process of fractional distillation	☺ 😐 ☹	☺ 😐 ☹	☺ 😐 ☹		TuitionKit http://bit.ly /2jGyD13
I can recall how boiling point changes with chain length	☺ 😐 ☹	☺ 😐 ☹	☺ 😐 ☹		
I can recall how viscosity changes with chain length	☺ 😐 ☹	☺ 😐 ☹	☺ 😐 ☹		
I can recall how flammability changes with chain length	☺ 😐 ☹	☺ 😐 ☹	☺ 😐 ☹		
I can recall the equation for complete combustion	☺ 😐 ☹	☺ 😐 ☹	☺ 😐 ☹	https://youtu.be/ Garj40Fyfuk	
I can describe the reasons why we need to crack long hydrocarbon chains	☺ 😐 ☹	☺ 😐 ☹	☺ 😐 ☹		TuitionKit http://bit.ly /2xew6ym

I can describe the process of cracking by steam and via a catalyst	☺ ☹ ☺	☺ ☹ ☺	☺ ☹ ☺		
I can describe the results of testing for alkenes with bromine water	☺ ☹ ☺	☺ ☹ ☺	☺ ☹ ☺	https://youtu.be/UQhyzisHawI	
I can recall and use the general formula for alkenes **Chemistry only**	☺ ☹ ☺	☺ ☹ ☺	☺ ☹ ☺	https://youtu.be/jFIWdxfQGMs	TuitionKit http://bit.ly/2wvPb2O
I can describe alkenes as unsaturated **Chemistry only**	☺ ☹ ☺	☺ ☹ ☺	☺ ☹ ☺		
I can name and draw the first four alkenes **Chemistry only**	☺ ☹ ☺	☺ ☹ ☺	☺ ☹ ☺	https://youtu.be/YNHKmgMKVI0	
I can recall the equation for incomplete combustion **Chemistry only**	☺ ☹ ☺	☺ ☹ ☺	☺ ☹ ☺	https://youtu.be/Garj4OFyfuk	
I can compare complete and incomplete combustions **Chemistry only**	☺ ☹ ☺	☺ ☹ ☺	☺ ☹ ☺		
I can describe the reaction of alkenes with hydrogen **Chemistry only**	☺ ☹ ☺	☺ ☹ ☺	☺ ☹ ☺		
I can describe the reaction of alkenes with water **Chemistry only**	☺ ☹ ☺	☺ ☹ ☺	☺ ☹ ☺		
I can describe the reaction of alkenes with the halogens **Chemistry only**	☺ ☹ ☺	☺ ☹ ☺	☺ ☹ ☺		
I can recall the functional group for alcohols **Chemistry only**	☺ ☹ ☺	☺ ☹ ☺	☺ ☹ ☺	https://youtu.be/DVY3YCpfNo4	TuitionKit http://bit.ly/2xOeCfk
I can name and draw the first four alcohols **Chemistry only**	☺ ☹ ☺	☺ ☹ ☺	☺ ☹ ☺		
I can recall the main uses for alcohols **Chemistry only**	☺ ☹ ☺	☺ ☹ ☺	☺ ☹ ☺		
I can describe what happens when alcohols react with sodium **Chemistry only**	☺ ☹ ☺	☺ ☹ ☺	☺ ☹ ☺		

I can describe what happens when alcohols react with oxygen **Chemistry only**	☺☻☹	☺☻☹	☺☻☹		
I can describe what happens when alcohols react with water **Chemistry only**	☺☻☹	☺☻☹	☺☻☹		
I can describe what happens when alcohols react with an oxidising agent **Chemistry only**	☺☻☹	☺☻☹	☺☻☹		
I can describe the conditions needed for fermentation **Chemistry only**	☺☻☹	☺☻☹	☺☻☹		
I can recall the functional group for carboxylic acids **Chemistry only**	☺☻☹	☺☻☹	☺☻☹	https://youtu.be/uIHoLv4_ZIg	TuitionKit http://bit.ly/2xedXAE
I can name and draw the first four carboxylic acids **Chemistry only**	☺☻☹	☺☻☹	☺☻☹	https://youtu.be/LG1PzsuDuck	
I can recall the main uses for carboxylic acids **Chemistry only**					
I can describe what happens when carboxylic acids react with carbonates **Chemistry only**	☺☻☹	☺☻☹	☺☻☹		
I can describe what happens when carboxylic acids react with water **Chemistry only**	☺☻☹	☺☻☹	☺☻☹		
I can describe what happens when carboxylic acids react with alcohols **Chemistry only**	☺☻☹	☺☻☹	☺☻☹		
I can name and draw ethyl ethanoate **Chemistry only**	☺☻☹	☺☻☹	☺☻☹		
I can define the terms monomer and polymer **Chemistry only**	☺☻☹	☺☻☹	☺☻☹		
I can explain the process of polymerisation **Chemistry only**	☺☻☹	☺☻☹	☺☻☹		

I can draw a polymer from a given monomer **Chemistry only**	☺ 😐 ☹	☺ 😐 ☹	☺ 😐 ☹		
I can draw the monomer from a given polymer **Chemistry only**	☺ 😐 ☹	☺ 😐 ☹	☺ 😐 ☹		
I can recall that condensation polymerisation involved monomers with different functional groups **Chemistry only** **Higher tier only**	☺ 😐 ☹	☺ 😐 ☹	☺ 😐 ☹		TuitionKit http://bit.ly /2xjMTlb
I can recall that condensation polymerisation involves the loss of a small molecules **Chemistry only** **Higher tier only**	☺ 😐 ☹	☺ 😐 ☹	☺ 😐 ☹		
I can explain the basic principles of condensation polymerisation **Chemistry only** **Higher tier only**	☺ 😐 ☹	☺ 😐 ☹	☺ 😐 ☹		
I can draw a polymer from a given monomer **Chemistry only** **Higher tier only**	☺ 😐 ☹	☺ 😐 ☹	☺ 😐 ☹		
I can draw the monomer from a given polymer **Chemistry only** **Higher tier only**	☺ 😐 ☹	☺ 😐 ☹	☺ 😐 ☹		
I can recall what DNA is **Chemistry only**	☺ 😐 ☹	☺ 😐 ☹	☺ 😐 ☹	https://youtu.be/ erZB_EhuKbA	TuitionKit http://bit.ly /2xjLcEd
I can recall the structure of DNA **Chemistry only**	☺ 😐 ☹	☺ 😐 ☹	☺ 😐 ☹		
I can recall how DNA relates to amino acids **Chemistry only**	☺ 😐 ☹	☺ 😐 ☹	☺ 😐 ☹		TuitionKit http://bit.ly /2fxiw1k
I can identify the two different functional groups in amino acid **Chemistry only**	☺ 😐 ☹	☺ 😐 ☹	☺ 😐 ☹		
I can describe how an amino acid polymerises **Chemistry only**	☺ 😐 ☹	☺ 😐 ☹	☺ 😐 ☹		

I can describe the process of amino acids joining together to form a polymer **Chemistry only**	☺ 😐 ☹	☺ 😐 ☹	☺ 😐 ☹		

Quick Fire Questions

This worksheet is fully supported by a video tutorial; https://youtu.be/sE2DP0x48kE

1. Define hydrocarbon.
2. What is crude oil made up from?
3. What is the general formula for alkanes?
4. Draw methane.
5. Draw ethane.
6. Draw propane.
7. Draw butane.
8. Why do we need to separate crude oil into fractions?
9. How does boiling point change with chain length?
10. How does viscosity change with chain length?
11. How does flammability change with chain length?
12. Write the word equation for complete combustion.
13. Why do we need to crack long hydrocarbons?
14. How do we test for alkenes?

Chemistry Only

15. What is the general formula for alkenes?
16. What does unsaturated mean?
17. Draw ethene.
18. Draw propene.
19. Draw butene.
20. Draw pentene.
21. What is the word equation for incomplete combustion?
22. What is the difference between complete and incomplete combustion?
23. Describe the reaction of an alkene with a halogen.
24. Describe the reaction of an alkene with water.
25. Describe the reaction of an alkene with hydrogen.
26. What is the functional group for alcohol?
27. Draw methanol.
28. Draw ethanol.
29. Draw propanol.
30. Draw butanol.
31. What is the main use of alcohol?
32. What happens when alcohol reacted oxygen?
33. What are the conditions needed for fermentation?

34. Draw the functional group for a carboxylic acid.
35. Draw methanoic acid.
36. Draw ethanoic acid.
37. Draw propanoic acid.
38. Draw butanoic acid.
39. What are the uses for carboxylic acids?
40. What happens when a carboxylic acid reacts with a carbonate?
41. What happens when a carboxylic acid reacts with water?
42. What happens when a carboxylic acid reacts with alcohol?
43. Draw ethyl ethanoate.
44. Define monomer.
45. Define polymer.
46. Describe polymerisation.
47. What is condensation polymerisation?
48. What is the structure of DNA?
49. How does DNA relate to amino acids?
50. Draw the basic structure of an amino acid.

8 – Chemical Analysis

Knowledge Checklist

Specification statement — These are the bits the exam board wants you to know, make sure you can do all of these…	Self-assessment			Bits to help if you don't understand	
	First review 4-7 months before exam	Second review 1-2 months before exam	Final review Week before exam	Primrose Kitten	Other places
I can recall the difference between a pure substance and a mixture	☺ 😐 ☹	☺ 😐 ☹	☺ 😐 ☹		TuitionKit http://bit.ly/2wuWTsX
I can define the term formulation	☺ 😐 ☹	☺ 😐 ☹	☺ 😐 ☹		
I can use the melting point of a substance to determine if it is pure or a mixture	☺ 😐 ☹	☺ 😐 ☹	☺ 😐 ☹		
I can give everyday example of formulations	☺ 😐 ☹	☺ 😐 ☹	☺ 😐 ☹		
I can describe how chromatography can be used to identify if a compound is pure or a mixture	☺ 😐 ☹	☺ 😐 ☹	☺ 😐 ☹		TuitionKit http://bit.ly/2ww3J1C
I can calculate R_f values	☺ 😐 ☹	☺ 😐 ☹	☺ 😐 ☹		
I can recall the test for hydrogen	☺ 😐 ☹	☺ 😐 ☹	☺ 😐 ☹	https://youtu.be/wuNB1n5z9QM	TuitionKit http://bit.ly/2ynX32F
I can recall the test for oxygen	☺ 😐 ☹	☺ 😐 ☹	☺ 😐 ☹		
I can recall the test for carbon dioxide	☺ 😐 ☹	☺ 😐 ☹	☺ 😐 ☹	https://youtu.be/QR6GsydYUSI	
I can recall the test for chlorine	☺ 😐 ☹	☺ 😐 ☹	☺ 😐 ☹		
I can recall the colours of the flame test (lithium, sodium, potassium, calcium, copper) **Chemistry only**	☺ 😐 ☹	☺ 😐 ☹	☺ 😐 ☹	https://youtu.be/i3fEVB9VN0Y https://youtu.be/LC4Nxd5dwEM	TuitionKit http://bit.ly/2he5l9f
I can recall the result for testing with sodium hydroxide (aluminium, calcium, magnesium, copper (II), iron (II), iron (III)) **Chemistry only**	☺ 😐 ☹	☺ 😐 ☹	☺ 😐 ☹	https://youtu.be/ESQYWh02Ykg	TuitionKit http://bit.ly/2xv04QR

I can write balanced equation for reactions with sodium hydroxide (aluminium, calcium, magnesium, copper (II), iron (II), iron (III)) **Chemistry only**	☺ 😐 ☹	☺ 😐 ☹	☺ 😐 ☹		
I can recall the test for carbonate ions **Chemistry only**	☺ 😐 ☹	☺ 😐 ☹	☺ 😐 ☹	https://youtu.be/7AGBLbl7AHE	TuitionKit http://bit.ly/2xcyLeo
I can recall the test for halide ions **Chemistry only**	☺ 😐 ☹	☺ 😐 ☹	☺ 😐 ☹	https://youtu.be/XtQ4hHZzX2k	
I can recall the test for sulfate ions **Chemistry only**	☺ 😐 ☹	☺ 😐 ☹	☺ 😐 ☹	https://youtu.be/k5qMGgmQDwo	
I can give the advantages and disadvantages of using instrumental method to identify ions rather than the ones used in class **Chemistry only**	☺ 😐 ☹	☺ 😐 ☹	☺ 😐 ☹		
I can describe the use of flame emission spectroscopy **Chemistry only**	☺ 😐 ☹	☺ 😐 ☹	☺ 😐 ☹		TuitionKit http://bit.ly/2yc7Fkq
I can interpret results of flame test emission spectroscopy **Chemistry only**	☺ 😐 ☹	☺ 😐 ☹	☺ 😐 ☹		

Quick Fire Questions.

This worksheet is fully supported by a video tutorial; https://youtu.be/vMKAHdoc-g0

1. Define mixture.
2. Defiant formulation.
3. Define melting point.
4. How can melting point be used to determine if a compound is pure or not?
5. How can chromatography be used to determine if a compound is pure or not?
6. How do you calculate R_f values?
7. What is the test for hydrogen gas?
8. What is the test oxygen gas?
9. What is the test for carbon dioxide?
10. What is the test for chlorine gas?

Chemistry only

11. What colour flame test for lithium go?
12. What colour flame test for sodium go?
13. What colour flame test for potassium go?
14. What colour flame test for calcium go?
15. What colour flame test for copper go?
16. What happens when you react aluminium with sodium hydroxide?
17. What happens when you react calcium with sodium hydroxide?
18. What happens when you react magnesium with sodium hydroxide?
19. What happens when you react copper (II) with sodium hydroxide?
20. What happens when you react iron (II) with sodium hydroxide?
21. What happens when you react iron (III) with sodium hydroxide?
22. What is the test carbonate ions?
23. What is the test for halide ions?
24. What is the test for sulfate ions?

9 – Chemistry of the Atmosphere

Knowledge Checklist

Specification statement — These are the bits the exam board wants you to know, make sure you can do all of these…	Self-assessment			Bits to help if you don't understand	
	First review 4-7 months before exam	Second review 1-2 months before exam	Final review Week before exam	Primrose Kitten	Other places
I can state the different proportions of the gases in the current atmosphere	☺ 😐 ☹	☺ 😐 ☹	☺ 😐 ☹	https://youtu.be/7IIF4Ydb5J0	TuitionKit http://bit.ly/2xOaI5Z
I can state that the Earth's atmosphere has changed over time	☺ 😐 ☹	☺ 😐 ☹	☺ 😐 ☹	https://youtu.be/EYeh1FhEmmU	TuitionKit http://bit.ly/2hg9VA9
I can describe that changes that have led to the evolution of today's atmosphere	☺ 😐 ☹	☺ 😐 ☹	☺ 😐 ☹	https://youtu.be/KMK8Bo6XdSc	
I can explain how the levels of oxygen increased	☺ 😐 ☹	☺ 😐 ☹	☺ 😐 ☹		TuitionKit http://bit.ly/2jI4tdX
I can explain how the levels of carbon dioxide decreased	☺ 😐 ☹	☺ 😐 ☹	☺ 😐 ☹		
I can state the greenhouse gases	☺ 😐 ☹	☺ 😐 ☹	☺ 😐 ☹	https://youtu.be/y5PZ1RN5mt0	TuitionKit http://bit.ly/2jJXD7R
I can describe how these gases interact with radiation	☺ 😐 ☹	☺ 😐 ☹	☺ 😐 ☹	https://youtu.be/9IvHkJxVukw	
I can describe the effect an increased level of these gases in the atmosphere has on the climate	☺ 😐 ☹	☺ 😐 ☹	☺ 😐 ☹	https://youtu.be/PK8aljEFRKA	
I can recall which activities contribute to increased levels of greenhouse gases in the atmosphere	☺ 😐 ☹	☺ 😐 ☹	☺ 😐 ☹	https://youtu.be/y5PZ1RN5mt0	TuitionKit http://bit.ly/2xvnWUr
I can recall what the predictions are for the effect of greenhouse gases of future temperature levels	☺ 😐 ☹	☺ 😐 ☹	☺ 😐 ☹		TuitionKit http://bit.ly/2f7QtF7

I can discuss the limitations of scientific models	☺ 😐 ☹	☺ 😐 ☹	☺ 😐 ☹		
I can define the term carbon footprint	☺ 😐 ☹	☺ 😐 ☹	☺ 😐 ☹		TuitionKit http://bit.ly/2f8AYq7
I can list the major sources of atmospheric pollution	☺ 😐 ☹	☺ 😐 ☹	☺ 😐 ☹		TuitionKit http://bit.ly/2xcvZFG
I can describe the effects that carbon dioxide has on the atmosphere	☺ 😐 ☹	☺ 😐 ☹	☺ 😐 ☹	https://youtu.be/PK8aljEFRKA	
I can describe the effects that sulfur dioxide has on the atmosphere	☺ 😐 ☹	☺ 😐 ☹	☺ 😐 ☹	https://youtu.be/nitv5kjgTKQ	
I can describe the effects that water vapour has on the atmosphere	☺ 😐 ☹	☺ 😐 ☹	☺ 😐 ☹		
I can describe the effects that carbon monoxide has on the atmosphere	☺ 😐 ☹	☺ 😐 ☹	☺ 😐 ☹		
I can describe the effects that nitrogen oxides have on the atmosphere	☺ 😐 ☹	☺ 😐 ☹	☺ 😐 ☹		
I can describe the effects that carbon particles have on the atmosphere	☺ 😐 ☹	☺ 😐 ☹	☺ 😐 ☹	https://youtu.be/Ut4xCQnSldM	
I can describe the effects that pollution has on humans, animals and plants	☺ 😐 ☹	☺ 😐 ☹	☺ 😐 ☹		

Quick Fire Questions

This worksheet is fully supported by a video tutorial; https://youtu.be/DznhhA2QHUg

1. How much oxygen is there in the atmosphere?
2. How much carbon dioxide is there in the atmosphere?
3. How much nitrogen is there in the atmosphere?
4. How was the early atmosphere different to todays?
5. What led to an increase in oxygen in the atmosphere?
6. What led to the increase in nitrogen in the atmosphere?
7. Give two things that led to a decrease in carbon dioxide in the atmosphere.
8. What are three greenhouse gases?
9. How do greenhouse gases interact with radiation?
10. What impact does increased level of these gases in the atmosphere have on the climate?
11. Give two activities that lead to an increased level of greenhouse gases in the atmosphere.
12. What are the predictions of the effects of greenhouse gases on future temperature levels?
13. Define the term carbon footprint.
14. What are the major sources of atmospheric pollution?
15. What affect does carbon dioxide have on the atmosphere?
16. What affect does sulfur dioxide have on the atmosphere?
17. What affect does water vapour have on the atmosphere?
18. What affect does carbon monoxide have on the atmosphere?
19. What affect does nitrogen oxides have on the atmosphere?
20. What affect do carbon particles have on the atmosphere?
21. What affect does pollution have on humans?
22. What affects does pollution have on plants?
23. What affect does pollution have on animals?

10 – Using Resources

Knowledge Checklist

Specification statement These are the bits the exam board wants you to know, make sure you can do all of these…	Self-assessment			Bits to help if you don't understand	
	First review 4-7 months before exam	Second review 1-2 months before exam	Final review Week before exam	Primrose Kitten	Other places
I can describe the different ways humans use the Earth's resources, including warmth, shelter, food and transport	☺ 😐 ☹	☺ 😐 ☹	☺ 😐 ☹		
I can state the resources we get from the Earth come from a range of sources including the land, oceans and atmosphere	☺ 😐 ☹	☺ 😐 ☹	☺ 😐 ☹		
I can differentiate between finite and renewable resources	☺ 😐 ☹	☺ 😐 ☹	☺ 😐 ☹		
I can state the importance of water to human life	☺ 😐 ☹	☺ 😐 ☹	☺ 😐 ☹		
I can recall the methods used to produce portable water	☺ 😐 ☹	☺ 😐 ☹	☺ 😐 ☹		TuitionKit http://bit.ly/2xPWWQg
I can describe the ways of sterilising water	☺ 😐 ☹	☺ 😐 ☹	☺ 😐 ☹		
I can describe the process of desalination	☺ 😐 ☹	☺ 😐 ☹	☺ 😐 ☹		
I can recall the difference between pure and portable water	☺ 😐 ☹	☺ 😐 ☹	☺ 😐 ☹		
I can describe the process of waste water treatment	☺ 😐 ☹	☺ 😐 ☹	☺ 😐 ☹	https://youtu.be/xJkKCzApbhM	TuitionKit http://bit.ly/2heNcnW
I can describe different method for purifying water	☺ 😐 ☹	☺ 😐 ☹	☺ 😐 ☹		

Statement					
I can explain the reasons for developing new method to extract metals from the Earth	☺☹☹	☺☹☹	☺☹☹		TuitionKit http://bit.ly/2fxzrkk
I can describe the process of bioleaching	☺☹☹	☺☹☹	☺☹☹		
I can describe the process of phytomining	☺☹☹	☺☹☹	☺☹☹		
I can assess the impact of raw materials, manufacturing, packaging, uses and disposal of an object	☺☹☹	☺☹☹	☺☹☹		
I can analyse Life Cycle Assessments	☺☹☹	☺☹☹	☺☹☹		
I can describe ways of reducing the amount of resources used.	☺☹☹	☺☹☹	☺☹☹		TuitionKit http://bit.ly/2yby6Xr
I can describe the process of rusting **Chemistry only**	☺☹☹	☺☹☹	☺☹☹	https://youtu.be/LQ-prcAHM_U	
I can describe ways to prevent corrosion **Chemistry only**	☺☹☹	☺☹☹	☺☹☹		TuitionKit http://bit.ly/2ycbHt4
I can interpret result that show which factors affect rusting **Chemistry only**	☺☹☹	☺☹☹	☺☹☹	https://youtu.be/LQ-prcAHM_U	
I can describe the structure of an alloy **Chemistry only**	☺☹☹	☺☹☹	☺☹☹		TuitionKit http://bit.ly/2w4OI2c
I can describe how the structure of an alloy relates to its properties **Chemistry only**	☺☹☹	☺☹☹	☺☹☹		
I can state the composition of most of the glass we use **Chemistry only**	☺☹☹	☺☹☹	☺☹☹		
I can describe the makeup of clay ceramics **Chemistry only**	☺☹☹	☺☹☹	☺☹☹		TuitionKit http://bit.ly/2xcGuZF
I can link the properties of polymers to their structure **Chemistry only**	☺☹☹	☺☹☹	☺☹☹	https://youtu.be/bPFn7Lehr6s	TuitionKit http://bit.ly/2xfeKRG
I can define the term composite and describe some uses **Chemistry only**	☺☹☹	☺☹☹	☺☹☹		

I can recall what the Haber process is used for **Chemistry only**	☺ 😐 ☹	☺ 😐 ☹	☺ 😐 ☹	https://youtu.be/0Yz1EgqfxAk	TuitionKit http://bit.ly/2ybTlYX
I can state the source of nitrogen and hydrogen **Chemistry only**	☺ 😐 ☹	☺ 😐 ☹	☺ 😐 ☹	https://youtu.be/sqq8iSFH4KU	
I can state the conditions needed for the Haber process **Chemistry only**	☺ 😐 ☹	☺ 😐 ☹	☺ 😐 ☹		
I can apply the principles of dynamic equilibrium to the Haber process **Chemistry only**	☺ 😐 ☹	☺ 😐 ☹	☺ 😐 ☹		
I can describe the production and uses of NPK fertilisers **Chemistry only**	☺ 😐 ☹	☺ 😐 ☹	☺ 😐 ☹		TuitionKit http://bit.ly/2wFjb6E

Quick Fire Question

This worksheet is fully supported by a video tutorial; https://youtu.be/xBUXqfa2gHo

1. What different ways can humans use the Earth's resources?
2. Give 3 resources we get from the Earth.
3. Define finite resource.
4. Define renewable resource.
5. How do you produce portable water?
6. How do you sterilise water?
7. How do you desalinate water?
8. Why do we need to develop new methods to extract materials from the Earth?
9. What is bioleaching?
10. What is phytomining?
11. How do we assess the impact of an object?
12. How do we analyse a life-cycle assessment?
13. How can you reduce amount of resources used?

Chemistry Only

14. What is rusting?
15. How can we prevent corrosion?
16. What is the structure of an alloy?
17. How does the structure of an ally relate to its properties?
18. What is the composition of most of the glass we use?
19. What are clay ceramics?
20. How do the structure of polymers link to their properties?
21. What is the Haber process used for?
22. In the Haber process, where does the nitrogen and hydrogen come from?
23. In the Haber process, what are the conditions needed?

Crosswords

Chemistry Crossword 1

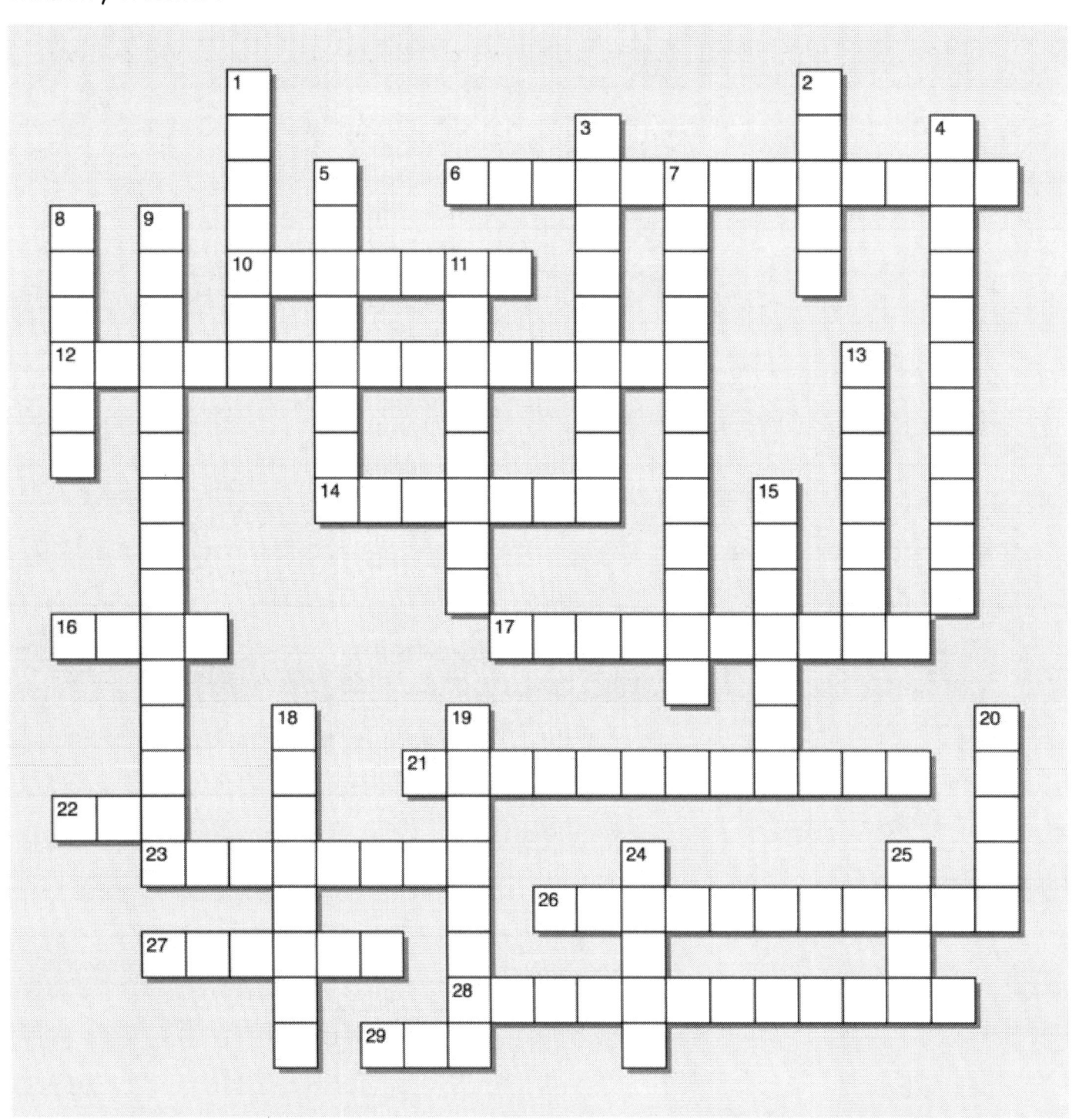

Across

6) a way of sorting out the elements

10) group of (or single) atoms that all have the same chemical characteristics, can be found on the periodic table

12) group of metal that are in the middle of the periodic table, form colour compounds and can be used as catalysts

14) found in the nucleus of atoms, has no charge and a mass of one

16) small part of matter, made up from a mixture of protons, neutrons and electrons

17) the number of protons and neutrons in an atom

21) transfer of electrons between a metal and a non-metal

22) atoms that has lost or gained electrons

23) giant covalent compound where each carbon atom makes three bonds

26) a way of determining how many of the reactant atoms made it into the desired product

27) a state of matter, where the atoms can move and flow but they cannot be compressed

28) the number of protons in an atom

29) a state of matter where the atoms move atom in a fast and random matter, can be compressed and flow

Down

1) in the centre of atoms, contains the protons and the neutrons

2) on the left-hand side of the periodic table, form positive ions

3) method for determining concentration of solution

4) highly reactive metals found on the left-hand side of the periodic table

5) found in the shells around the nucleus, has a charge of minus one and no mass

7) a type of reaction where one element replaces another in a compound

8) found in the nucleus of atoms, has a charge of plus one and a mass of one

9) sharing of electron between two non-metals

11) on the right-hand side of the periodic table, form negative ions

13) lots of different elements that may or may not be chemically bonded together

15) giant covalent compound where each carbon atom makes four bonds

18) two or more elements chemically bonded together

19) unreactive gases found on the right of the periodic table

20) mixture of atoms that lead to distorted layers that cannot slide

24) a state of matter, where the atoms vibrate around a fixed position

25) the molecular mass in grams

Chemistry Crossword 2

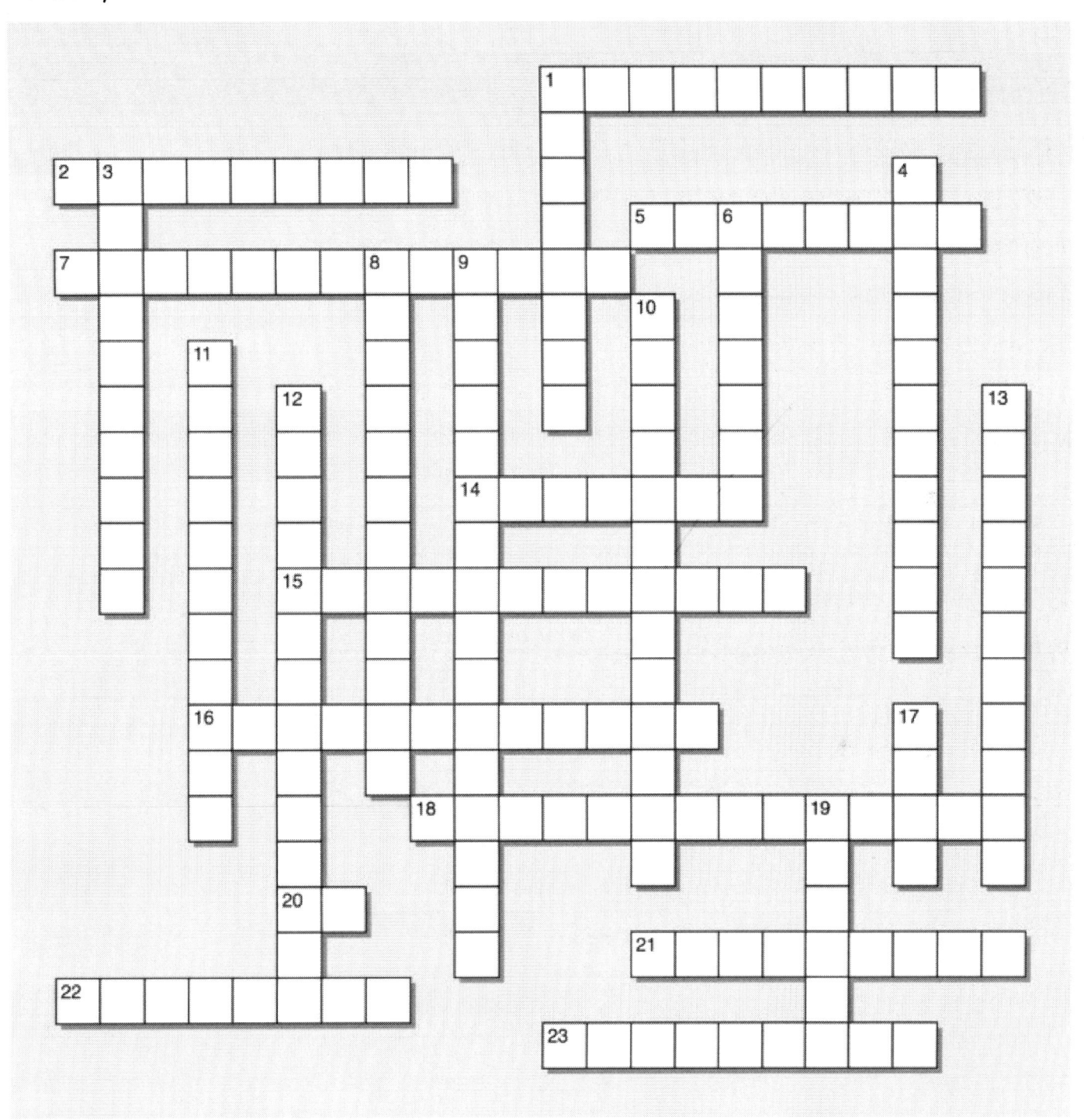

Across

1) burning of a compound in oxygen

2) gain of electrons

5) breaking a long hydrocarbon chain to short hydrocarbon chains

7) water that is safe to drink

14) hydrocarbon containing double bonds

15) point at which a solid turns into a liquid

16) orange liquid that can be used to test for double bonds

18) mixing of an acid and an alkali to give a pH of 7

20) how acid or alkali a solution is

21) loss of electrons

22) something that speeds up a react of reaction without being use dup

23) how easily pourable something is

Down

1) a mixture of different length hydrocarbon chains made from decomposing dead plant and animals

3) a reaction that releases energy

4) a reaction that takes in energy

6) hydrocarbon containing only single bonds

8) separating compounds using electricity

9) the energy needed to start reaction

10) gas that traps infra-red radiation

11) a compound that only has carbon and hydrogen in it

12) method of separating out mixtures

13) mining low yield ores using plants

17) a solution that has a low pH due to the hydrogen ions

19) a solution that has a high pH due to hydroxide ions

Physics

5 most common mistakes in a physics exam

1. Not knowing your units - this comes up a lot as separate marks and your formula sheet will be useless if don't know these
2. Not being able to rearrange equations - if you want to get the top grades you'll need to use sophisticated maths skills
3. We don't use reoccurring in science - you need to round to the nearest whole number
4. Store numbers in your calculator's memory - so you don't make an error due to rounding
5. Missing out the keywords – easy, easy makes here but you need to learn them!!

Topic Guide

Topic	First review	Second review	Third review
1 - Energy			
2 - Electricity			
3 - Particle Model of Matter			
4 - Atomic Structure			
5 - Forces			
6 - Waves			
7 - Magnetism and Electromagnets			
8 - Space Physics			

Topic	Quick fire questions	Whole topic summary
1 – Energy	https://youtu.be/q5CwATii6OA	
2 – Electricity	https://youtu.be/62RyyfKZoYg	
3 – Particle Model of Matter	https://youtu.be/z9L6zfMVk3U	https://youtu.be/cZz9oGqJOL0
4 – Atomic Structure	https://youtu.be/bRzRjfvoU-E	
5 – Forces	https://youtu.be/jfjb1pnH8zw	
6 – Waves	https://youtu.be/AEFwEDC6DkQ	
7 – Magnetism and Electromagnets	https://youtu.be/LyflUYL4FvM	
8 – Space Physics	https://youtu.be/f3Rf1aVStIk	https://youtu.be/Mdi0i24tNT0

Required practical's

1. Specific Heat Capacity
2. Thermal Insulation (Physics only)
3. Resistance
4. I-V characteristics
5. Density
6. Forces
7. Acceleration
8. Waves
9. Reflection (Physics only)
10. Surfaces

https://youtu.be/kDLx36gDz80

AQA GCSE Physics Equation Sheet

Units and equations available as readymade flashcards from my website

Topic 1 – Energy

Equation	Symbol	Unit
$E_k = \frac{1}{2}mv^2$	E_k = kinetic energy m = mass v = speed	E_k = J (joules) m = kg (kilograms) v = m/s (meters per second)
$E_e = \frac{1}{2}ke^2$	E_e = elastic potential energy k = spring constant e = extension	E_e = J (joules) k = N/m (newtons per meter) e = m (meters)
$E_p = mgh$	E_p = gravitational potential energy m = mass g = gravitational field strength h = height	E_p = J (joules) m = kg (kilograms) g = N/kg (newtons per kilogram) h = m (meters)
$\Delta E = mc\Delta\theta$	ΔE = change in thermal energy m = mass c = specific heat capacity $\Delta\theta$ = temperature change	ΔE = J (joules) m = kg (kilograms) c = J/kg°C (joules per kilogram degree Celsius) $\Delta\theta$ = °C (degree Celsius)
$P = \frac{E}{T}$	P = power E = energy transferred t = time	P = W (watts) E = J (joules) t = s (seconds)
$P = \frac{W}{T}$	P = power W = work done t = time	P = W (watts) E = J (joules) t = s (seconds)
Efficiency = $\frac{\text{useful energy out}}{\text{total energy in}}$		
Efficiency = $\frac{\text{useful power out}}{\text{total power in}}$		

Topic 2 – Electricity

Equation	Symbols	Units
$Q = It$	Q = Charge I = Current t = Time	Q = C (coulombs) I = A (amps) t = s (seconds)
$V = IR$	V = Potential difference I = Current R = Resistance	V = V (volts) I = A (amps) R = Ω (ohms)
$P = VI$	P = Power V = Potential difference I = Current	P = W (watts) V = V (volts) I = A (amps)
$P = I^2R$	P = Power I = Current R = Resistance	P = W (watts) I = A (amps) R = Ω (ohms)
$E = Pt$	E = Energy P = Power t = Time	E = J (joules) P = W (watts) t = s (seconds)
$E = QV$	E = Energy Q = Charge V = Potential difference	E = J (joules) Q = C (coulombs) V = V (volts)

Topic 3 – Particle Model of Matter

Equation	Symbols	Units
$\rho = \dfrac{m}{V}$	ρ = density m = mass V = volume	ρ = kg/m³ (kilograms per meter cubed) m = kg (kilograms) V = m³ (meters cubed)
$\Delta E = mc\Delta\theta$	ΔE = change in thermal energy m = mass c = specific heat capacity Δθ = temperature change	ΔE = J (joules) m = kg (kilograms) c = J/kg°C (joules per kilogram degree Celsius) Δθ = °C (degree Celsius)
$E = mL$	E = Energy m = mass L = specific latent heat	E = J (joules) m = kg (kilograms) L = J/kg (joules per kilogram)
$pV = \text{constant}$	p = pressure V = volume	p = Pa (pascals) V = m³ (meters cubed)

Topic 5 – Forces

Equation	Symbols	Units
$W = mg$	W = weight m = mass g = gravitational field strength	W = N (newton's) m = kg (kilograms) g = N/kg (newtons per kilogram)
$W = Fs$	W = work done F = force s = distance	W = J (joules) F = N (newtons) s = m (meters)
$F = ke$	F = force k = spring constant e = extension	F = N (newtons) k = N/m (newtons per meter) e = m (meters)
$E_e = \frac{1}{2} ke^2$	E_e = elastic potential energy k = spring constant e = extension	E_e = J (joules) k = N/m (newtons per meter) e = m (meters)
$M = Fd$	M = moment F = force d = distance	M = Nm (newton-meters) F = N (newtons) d = m (meters)
$p = \dfrac{F}{A}$	p = pressure F = force A = area	p = Pa (pascals) F = N (newtons) A = m² (meters squared)
$p = h\rho g$	p = pressure h = height ρ = density g = gravitational field strength	p = Pa (pascals) h = m (meters) ρ = kg/m³ (kilograms per meter cubed) g = N/kg (newtons per kilogram)
$s = vt$	s = distance v = speed t = time	s = m (meters) v = m/s (meters per second) t = s (seconds)
$a = \dfrac{\Delta v}{t}$	a = acceleration Δv = change in velocity t = time	a = m/s² (meters per second squared) Δv = m/s (meters per second) t = s (seconds)
$v^2 - u^2 = 2as$	v = final velocity u = initial velocity a = acceleration s = distance	v = m/s (meters per second) u = m/s (meters per second) a = m/s² (meters per second squared) s = m (meters)

Equation	Symbols	Units
$F = ma$	F = force m = mass a = acceleration	F = N (newtons) m = kg (kilograms) a = m/s² (meters per second squared)
$p = mv$	p = momentum m = mass v = velocity	p = kg m/s (kilograms metre per second) m = kg (kilograms) v = m/s (meters per second)
$F = \dfrac{m \Delta v}{\Delta t}$	F = force m = mass v = velocity t = time	F = N (newtons) m = kg (kilograms) v = m/s (meters per second) t = s (seconds)

Topic 6 – Waves

Equation	Symbols	Units
Period = $\dfrac{1}{\text{Frequency}}$		Period = s (seconds) Frequency = Hz (hertz)
$T = \dfrac{1}{F}$	T = Period f = frequency	T = s (seconds) f = Hz (hertz)
$v = f\lambda$	v = velocity f = frequency λ = wavelength (lambda)	v = m/s (meters per second) f = Hz (hertz) λ = m (meters)
Magnification = $\dfrac{\text{image height}}{\text{object height}}$		Ratio, so has no units

Topic 7 – Magnetism and Electromagnetism

Equation	Symbols	Units
$F = BIl$ Note this is a capital I and a lowercase l	F = force B = magnetic flux density I = Current l = length	F = N (newtons) B = T (tesla) I = A (Amps or Amperes) l = m (meters)
$\dfrac{V_p}{V_s} = \dfrac{n_p}{n_s}$	V_p = potential difference across the primary coil V_s = potential difference across the secondary coil n_p = number of turns on the primary coil n_s = number of turns on the secondary coil	V_p = V (volts) V_s = V (volts) n_p and n_s have no units as they are just numbers
$V_s I_s = V_p I_p$	V_s = potential difference across the secondary coil V_p = potential difference across the primary coil I_s = current in the secondary coil I_p = current in the primary coil $V_s I_s$ = power output $V_p I_p$ = power input	V_s = V (volts) V_p = V (volts) I_s = A (Amps or Amperes) I_p = A (Amps or Amperes)

1 – Energy

Knowledge Checklist

Specification statement These are the bits the exam board wants you to know, make sure you can do all of these…	Self-assessment			Bits to help if you don't understand	
	First review 4-7 months before exam	Second review 1-2 months before exam	Final review Week before exam	Primrose Kitten	Other places
I can recall the different types of energy and give examples	☺ 😐 ☹	☺✓ 😐 ☹	☺ 😐 ☹	https://youtu.be/ujdUEwMfIok https://youtu.be/nd97wwioCX4	
I can describe the energy changes involved in a range of common situations	☺ 😐 ☹	☺✓ 😐 ☹	☺ 😐 ☹		
I can define the term system	☺ 😐 ☹	☺✓ 😐 ☹	☺ 😐 ☹		
I can recall that energy cannot be created or destroyed	☺ 😐 ☹	☺✓ 😐 ☹	☺ 😐 ☹		
I can use describe how kinetic energy changes over time	☺ 😐 ☹	☺ 😐 ☹	☺ 😐 ☹		
I can recall the units needed for $E_k = \frac{1}{2}mv^2$	☺ 😐 ☹	☺✓ 😐 ☹	☺ 😐 ☹	https://youtu.be/RRm_8BDgH1M	Flashcards available on www.primrosekitten.com
I can rearrange $E_k = \frac{1}{2}mv^2$	☺ 😐 ☹	☺ 😐 ☹	☺ 😐 ☹		
I can use $E_k = \frac{1}{2}mv^2$	☺ 😐 ☹	☺ 😐 ☹	☺ 😐 ☹		
I can use describe how elastic potential energy changes	☺ 😐 ☹	☺ 😐 ☹	☺ 😐 ☹		
I can recall the units needed for $E_e = \frac{1}{2}ke^2$	☺ 😐 ☹	☺ 😐 ☹	☺ 😐 ☹		Flashcards available on www.primrosekitten.com
I can rearrange $E_e = \frac{1}{2}ke^2$	☺ 😐 ☹	☺ 😐 ☹	☺ 😐 ☹		
I can use $E_e = \frac{1}{2}ke^2$	☺ 😐 ☹	☺ 😐 ☹	☺ 😐 ☹		
I can use describe how gravitational potential energy changes	☺ 😐 ☹	☺ 😐 ☹	☺ 😐 ☹		

I can recall the units needed for $E_p = mgh$	☺ 😐 ☹	☺ 😐 ☹	☺ 😐 ☹		Flashcards available on www.primrosekitten.com
I can rearrange $E_p = mgh$	☺ 😐 ☹	☺ 😐 ☹	☺ 😐 ☹		
I can use $E_p = mgh$	☺ 😐 ☹	☺ 😐 ☹	☺ 😐 ☹		
I can use describe how objects have different specific heat capacities	☺ 😐 ☹	☺ 😐 ☹	☺ 😐 ☹	https://youtu.be/_gooQFvVqzk	
I can recall the units needed for $\Delta E = mc\Delta\theta$	☺ 😐 ☹	☺ 😐 ☹	☺ 😐 ☹		Flashcards available on www.primrosekitten.com
I can rearrange $\Delta E = mc\Delta\theta$	☺ 😐 ☹	☺ 😐 ☹	☺ 😐 ☹		
I can use $\Delta E = mc\Delta\theta$	☺ 😐 ☹	☺ 😐 ☹	☺ 😐 ☹		
I can use define power	☺ 😐 ☹	☺ 😐 ☹	☺ 😐 ☹		
I can recall the units needed for $P = \frac{E}{T}$	☺ 😐 ☹	☺ 😐 ☹	☺ 😐 ☹		Flashcards available on www.primrosekitten.com
I can rearrange $P = \frac{E}{T}$	☺ 😐 ☹	☺ 😐 ☹	☺ 😐 ☹		
I can use $P = \frac{E}{T}$	☺ 😐 ☹	☺ 😐 ☹	☺ 😐 ☹		
I can recall the units needed for $P = \frac{W}{T}$	☺ 😐 ☹	☺ 😐 ☹	☺ 😐 ☹		Flashcards available on www.primrosekitten.com
I can rearrange $P = \frac{W}{T}$	☺ 😐 ☹	☺ 😐 ☹	☺ 😐 ☹		
I can use $P = \frac{W}{T}$	☺ 😐 ☹	☺ 😐 ☹	☺ 😐 ☹		
I can recall that energy cannot be created or destroyed	☺ 😐 ☹	☺ 😐 ☹	☺ 😐 ☹		
I can describe what happen to wasted energy	☺ 😐 ☹	☺ 😐 ☹	☺ 😐 ☹		
I can recall ways to reduce wasted energy	☺ 😐 ☹	☺ 😐 ☹	☺ 😐 ☹		
I can describe how insulation can reduce energy loss	☺ 😐 ☹	☺ 😐 ☹	☺ 😐 ☹		

I can describe why a system might not be 100% efficient	☺ 😐 ☹	☺ 😐 ☹	☺ 😐 ☹		
I can describe whys to increase the efficiency of a system	☺ 😐 ☹	☺ 😐 ☹	☺ 😐 ☹		
I can recall the units needed for $$\text{Efficiency} = \frac{\text{useful energy out}}{\text{total energy in}}$$	☺ 😐 ☹	☺ 😐 ☹	☺ 😐 ☹	https://youtu.be/GVSiL39bnrc	
I can rearrange $$\text{Efficiency} = \frac{\text{useful energy out}}{\text{total energy in}}$$	☺ 😐 ☹	☺ 😐 ☹	☺ 😐 ☹		
I can use $$\text{Efficiency} = \frac{\text{useful energy out}}{\text{total energy in}}$$	☺ 😐 ☹	☺ 😐 ☹	☺ 😐 ☹		
I can recall the units needed for $$\text{Efficiency} = \frac{\text{useful power out}}{\text{total power in}}$$	☺ 😐 ☹	☺ 😐 ☹	☺ 😐 ☹		
I can rearrange $$\text{Efficiency} = \frac{\text{useful power out}}{\text{total power in}}$$	☺ 😐 ☹	☺ 😐 ☹	☺ 😐 ☹		
I can use $$\text{Efficiency} = \frac{\text{useful power out}}{\text{total power in}}$$	☺ 😐 ☹	☺ 😐 ☹	☺ 😐 ☹		
I can state the different sources that can be used to get energy	☺ 😐 ☹	☺ 😐 ☹	☺ 😐 ☹		
I can determine if a resource is renewable or finite	☺ 😐 ☹	☺ 😐 ☹	☺ 😐 ☹		
I can consider the impact that using these resources has on the environment	☺ 😐 ☹	☺ 😐 ☹	☺ 😐 ☹		
I can discuss the advantages and disadvantages of each source of energy	☺ 😐 ☹	☺ 😐 ☹	☺ 😐 ☹		

Quick fire questions;

This worksheet is fully supported by a video tutorial; https://youtu.be/q5CwATii6OA

1. What are the different types of energy?
2. What energy changes happen in a lightbulb?
3. What energy changes happen in TV?
4. What does the word system mean?
5. What is the law of conservation of energy?
6. What is the equation linking kinetic energy, mass and velocity?
7. What are the units for velocity?
8. What are the units for mass?
9. What are the units for kinetic energy?
10. What is elastic potential energy?
11. What is equation linking elastic potential energy, the spring constant and extension?
12. What are units for elastic potential energy?
13. What are the units for the spring constant?
14. What are the units for extension?
15. What is gravitational potential energy?
16. What is the equation linking gravitational potential energy, mass, gravity and height?
17. What are the units for gravitational potential energy?
18. What is the value and the units for gravity?
19. What are the units for height?
20. What does this symbol mean Δ?
21. What is specific heat capacity?
22. What is the equation linking changing energy, mass, specific heat capacity and change in temperature?
23. What are the units for energy?
24. What are the units for specific heat capacity?
25. What are the units for change in temperature?
26. What is the equation linking power, energy and time?
27. What are the units of power?
28. What are the units for time?
29. What is the equation linking power, work done and time?
30. What are the units for work done?
31. What happens to waste energy?

32. How can we reduce wasting energy?
33. Give three examples of insulation that can be used in the house.
34. Why is a system not 100% efficient?
35. What is the equation for working out efficiency?
36. What are the units for efficiency?
37. What different ways we can get energy?
38. What is a renewable resource?
39. What is finite resource?

2 – Electricity

Knowledge Checklist

Specification statement These are the bits the exam board wants you to know, make sure you can do all of these...	Self-assessment			Bits to help if you don't understand	
	First review 4-7 months before exam	Second review 1-2 months before exam	Final review Week before exam	Primrose Kitten	Other places
I can draw and use the common circuit symbols	☺ 😐 ☹	☺ 😐 ☹	☺ 😐 ☹		Circuit symbol flashcard on www.primrosekitten.com
I can draw series and parallel circuits	☺ 😐 ☹	☺ 😐 ☹	☺ 😐 ☹	https://youtu.be/2QBTag63mYk https://youtu.be/rbLqufYEVN8 https://youtu.be/xZXKaQW2jBc https://youtu.be/oBuewt6m_KM	
I can define the terms charge and current	☺ 😐 ☹	☺ 😐 ☹	☺ 😐 ☹	https://youtu.be/k3vCg3lGpys	
I can recall the units needed for Q = It	☺ 😐 ☹	☺ 😐 ☹	☺ 😐 ☹		Flashcards available on www.primrosekitten.com
I can rearrange Q = It	☺ 😐 ☹	☺ 😐 ☹	☺ 😐 ☹		
I can use Q = It	☺ 😐 ☹	☺ 😐 ☹	☺ 😐 ☹		
I can define the terms potential difference and resistance	☺ 😐 ☹	☺ 😐 ☹	☺ 😐 ☹	https://youtu.be/k3vCg3lGpys	

Primrose Kitten – YouTube Tutorials for Science and Maths.

I can recall the units needed for V = IR	☺ 😐 ☹	☺ 😐 ☹	☺ 😐 ☹		Flashcards available on www.primrosekitten.com
I can rearrange V = IR	☺ 😐 ☹	☺ 😐 ☹	☺ 😐 ☹		
I can use V = IR	☺ 😐 ☹	☺ 😐 ☹	☺ 😐 ☹		
I can draw and explain current-potential difference graphs for ohmic conductors, filament lamps and diodes	☺ 😐 ☹	☺ 😐 ☹	☺ 😐 ☹	https://youtu.be/fxDNgQ3hH2A https://youtu.be/ylHsTMAGV1I	
I can explain the change in resistance of a thermistor as the temperature changes	☺ 😐 ☹	☺ 😐 ☹	☺ 😐 ☹	https://youtu.be/2PdHk4wa5Bg https://youtu.be/Ra7sqF8oZxg	
I can explain the change in resistance of an LDR as the light intensity changes	☺ 😐 ☹	☺ 😐 ☹	☺ 😐 ☹	https://youtu.be/Ra7sqF8oZxg https://youtu.be/iUnMBMmkxnY	
I can describe the way current behaves in a series circuit	☺ 😐 ☹	☺ 😐 ☹	☺ 😐 ☹	https://youtu.be/g2kUj3xfM90 https://youtu.be/E70eNm2lITI https://youtu.be/OdmmKxa0Nhs	https://phet.colorado.edu/en/simulation/legacy/circuit-construction-kit-ac-virtual-lab
I can describe the way potential difference behaves in a series circuit	☺ 😐 ☹	☺ 😐 ☹	☺ 😐 ☹		
I can describe the way resistance behaves in a series circuit	☺ 😐 ☹	☺ 😐 ☹	☺ 😐 ☹		
I can describe the way current behaves in a parallel circuit	☺ 😐 ☹	☺ 😐 ☹	☺ 😐 ☹	https://youtu.be/g2kUj3xfM90	https://phet.colorado.edu/en/simulation/legacy/circuit-construction-kit-ac-virtual-lab
I can describe the way potential difference behaves in a parallel circuit	☺ 😐 ☹	☺ 😐 ☹	☺ 😐 ☹		

I can describe the way resistance behaves in a parallel circuit	☺ 😐 ☹	☺ 😐 ☹	☺ 😐 ☹		
I can recall the voltage and frequency of mains electricity in the UK	☺ 😐 ☹	☺ 😐 ☹	☺ 😐 ☹		
I can explain the difference between direct current and alternating current	☺ 😐 ☹	☺ 😐 ☹	☺ 😐 ☹		
I can describe the inside of a plug	☺ 😐 ☹	☺ 😐 ☹	☺ 😐 ☹	https://youtu.be/Ke4yyUZH-hY	
I can describe the safety features of a plug	☺ 😐 ☹	☺ 😐 ☹	☺ 😐 ☹		
I can describe how power in a circuit is related to the potential difference	☺ 😐 ☹	☺ 😐 ☹	☺ 😐 ☹		
I can recall the units needed for $P = VI$	☺ 😐 ☹	☺ 😐 ☹	☺ 😐 ☹		Flashcards available on www.primrosekitten.com
I can rearrange $P = VI$	☺ 😐 ☹	☺ 😐 ☹	☺ 😐 ☹		
I can use $P = VI$	☺ 😐 ☹	☺ 😐 ☹	☺ 😐 ☹		
I can recall the units needed for $P = I^2R$	☺ 😐 ☹	☺ 😐 ☹	☺ 😐 ☹		Flashcards available on www.primrosekitten.com
I can rearrange $P = I^2R$	☺ 😐 ☹	☺ 😐 ☹	☺ 😐 ☹		
I can use $P = I^2R$	☺ 😐 ☹	☺ 😐 ☹	☺ 😐 ☹		
I can describe how domestic appliances transfer energy	☺ 😐 ☹	☺ 😐 ☹	☺ 😐 ☹		
I can recall the units needed for $E = Pt$	☺ 😐 ☹	☺ 😐 ☹	☺ 😐 ☹		Flashcards available on www.primrosekitten.com
I can rearrange $E = Pt$	☺ 😐 ☹	☺ 😐 ☹	☺ 😐 ☹		
I can use $E = Pt$	☺ 😐 ☹	☺ 😐 ☹	☺ 😐 ☹		
I can recall the units needed for $E = QV$	☺ 😐 ☹	☺ 😐 ☹	☺ 😐 ☹		Flashcards available on www.primrosekitten.com
I can rearrange $E = QV$	☺ 😐 ☹	☺ 😐 ☹	☺ 😐 ☹		
I can use $E = QV$	☺ 😐 ☹	☺ 😐 ☹	☺ 😐 ☹		

I can describe the part of the National Grid and how they interact with each other	☺ 😐 ☹	☺ 😐 ☹	☺ 😐 ☹		
I can describe how step-up and step-down transformers work	☺ 😐 ☹	☺ 😐 ☹	☺ 😐 ☹		
I can describe the circumstances in which an object might become charged **-Physics only**	☺ 😐 ☹	☺ 😐 ☹	☺ 😐 ☹		
I can describe what happens what two charged objects are bought close together **-Physics only**	☺ 😐 ☹	☺ 😐 ☹	☺ 😐 ☹		
I can state that a charged object creates an electric field around itself **-Physics only**	☺ 😐 ☹	☺ 😐 ☹	☺ 😐 ☹		
I can draw the electric field pattern for an object **-Physics only**	☺ 😐 ☹	☺ 😐 ☹	☺ 😐 ☹		

Quick fire questions;

This worksheet is fully supported by a video tutorial; https://youtu.be/62RyyfKZoYg

1. Draw the symbol for a cell.
2. Draw the symbol for a battery.
3. What is the difference between a battery and a cell?
4. Draw the symbol for an ammeter.
5. How must an ammeter be placed in a circuit?
6. Draw the symbol for a voltmeter.
7. How must a voltmeter be placed in a circuit?
8. Draw the symbol for a lamp.
9. Draw the symbol for a diode.
10. Draw the symbol for a resistor.
11. Draw the symbol for a LED (light emitting diodes).
12. Draw the symbol for a variable resistor.
13. Draw the symbol for a LDR (light dependent resistor).
14. Draw the symbol for a fuse.
15. Draw the symbol for a thermistor.
16. Draw the symbol for an open switch.
17. Draw the symbol for a closed switch.
18. What is difference between series and parallel circuits?
19. Define charge.
20. Define current.
21. What is equation taking charge, current and time?
22. What are the units for charge?
23. What are the units for current?
24. What are the units for time?
25. Define potential difference.
26. Define resistance.
27. What is equation linking potential difference, current and resistance?
28. What are the units of potential difference?
29. What are the units for resistance?
30. Draw the current-potential different graphs for a conductor.
31. Draw the current-potential different graphs for lamp.
32. Draw the current-potential different graphs for a diode.
33. How does resistance of a thermistor change as temperature changes?
34. How does resistance of an LDR change as light intensity changes?
35. How does current behave in a series circuit?

36. How does potential difference behave in a series circuit?
37. How does resistance behave in a series circuit?
38. How does current behave in a parallel circuit?
39. How does potential difference behave in a parallel circuit?
40. How does resistance behave in a parallel circuit?
41. What is the voltage of mains electricity in the UK?
42. What is the frequency of mains electricity in the UK?
43. What is the difference between alternating and direct current?
44. What are the three wires inside a plug?
45. What are the safety features on a plug?
46. What is equation linking power, current and potential difference?
47. What are the units for power?
48. What is the equation linking power, current and resistance?
49. What is equation linking energy, power and time?
50. What are the units for energy?
51. What are the units for time?
52. What is equation linking energy, charge and potential difference?
53. What is the National Grid?
54. What does step up transformer do?
55. What does a step-down transformer do?

3 - Particle Model of Matter

Knowledge Checklist

Whole topic summary video; https://youtu.be/cZz9oGgJOL0 only 6 minutes!

Specification statement These are the bits the exam board wants you to know, make sure you can do all of these...	Self-assessment			Bits to help if you don't understand	
	First review 4-7 months before exam	Second review 1-2 months before exam	Final review Week before exam	Primrose Kitten	Other places
I can recall the arrangement of particles in a solid, a liquid and a gas	☺ 😐 ☹	☺ 😐 ☹	☺ 😐 ☹	https://youtu.be/hs9DIOqzgRg	
I can describe the energy changes that happen when a substance changes state	☺ 😐 ☹	☺ 😐 ☹	☺ 😐 ☹		
I can describe the energy in the atoms and molecules as internal energy	☺ 😐 ☹	☺ 😐 ☹	☺ 😐 ☹		
I can explain that a change in the internal energy will lead to a change in temperature or a change in state	☺ 😐 ☹	☺ 😐 ☹	☺ 😐 ☹		
I can define density	☺ 😐 ☹	☺ 😐 ☹	☺ 😐 ☹		
I can recall the units needed for $\rho = \frac{m}{V}$	☺ 😐 ☹	☺ 😐 ☹	☺ 😐 ☹		Flashcards available on www.primrosekitten.com
I can rearrange $\rho = \frac{m}{V}$	☺ 😐 ☹	☺ 😐 ☹	☺ 😐 ☹		
I can use $\rho = \frac{m}{V}$	☺ 😐 ☹	☺ 😐 ☹	☺ 😐 ☹		
I can define specific heat capacity and specific latent heat	☺ 😐 ☹	☺ 😐 ☹	☺ 😐 ☹		
I can recall the units needed for $\Delta E = mc\Delta\theta$	☺ 😐 ☹	☺ 😐 ☹	☺ 😐 ☹		Flashcards available on www.primrosekitten.com

I can rearrange $\Delta E = mc\Delta\theta$	☺ 😐 ☹	☺ 😐 ☹	☺ 😐 ☹		
I can use $\Delta E = mc\Delta\theta$	☺ 😐 ☹	☺ 😐 ☹	☺ 😐 ☹		
I can recall the units needed for $E = mL$	☺ 😐 ☹	☺ 😐 ☹	☺ 😐 ☹		Flashcards available on www.primrose kitten.com
I can rearrange $E = mL$	☺ 😐 ☹	☺ 😐 ☹	☺ 😐 ☹		
I can use $E = mL$	☺ 😐 ☹	☺ 😐 ☹	☺ 😐 ☹		
I can describe the movement of particles in a gas	☺ 😐 ☹	☺ 😐 ☹	☺ 😐 ☹		
I can relate the temperature of the gas to the average kinetic energy of the system	☺ 😐 ☹	☺ 😐 ☹	☺ 😐 ☹		
I can explain how the motion of a gas relates to the pressure in a system	☺ 😐 ☹	☺ 😐 ☹	☺ 😐 ☹		
I can relate the volume of a gas to the pressure -**Physics only**	☺ 😐 ☹	☺ 😐 ☹	☺ 😐 ☹		
I can recall the units needed for pV = constant -**Physics only**	☺ 😐 ☹	☺ 😐 ☹	☺ 😐 ☹		Flashcards available on www.primrose kitten.com
I can rearrange pV = constant -**Physics only**	☺ 😐 ☹	☺ 😐 ☹	☺ 😐 ☹		
I can use pV = constant -**Physics only**	☺ 😐 ☹	☺ 😐 ☹	☺ 😐 ☹		
I can explain how doing work on a system can increase the temperature -**Physics only**	☺ 😐 ☹	☺ 😐 ☹	☺ 😐 ☹		

Quick fire questions;

This worksheet is fully supported by a video tutorial; https://youtu.be/z9L6zfMVk3U

1. Draw arrangement of particles in a solid.
2. Draw the arrangement of particles in liquid.
3. Draw the arrangement of particles in a gas.
4. Define density.
5. What is the equation linking density, mass and volume?
6. What are the units for density?
7. What are units the mass?
8. What are the units for volume?
9. What is specific heat capacity?
10. What is specific latent heat?
11. What is the equation linking energy change, mass, specific heat capacity and change in temperature?
12. What are the units for energy change?
13. What are the units for specific heat capacity?
14. What are the units for temperature change?
15. What is equation linking energy, mass and specific latent heat?
16. What are the units for specific latent heat?

Physics only

17. What is relationship between volume of gas and pressure?
18. What is the equation linking pressure, volume and the constant?
19. What are the units of pressure?

4 - Atomic Structure

Knowledge Checklist

Specification statement These are the bits the exam board wants you to know, make sure you can do all of these...	Self-assessment			Bits to help if you don't understand	
	First review 4-7 months before exam	Second review 1-2 months before exam	Final review Week before exam	Primrose Kitten	Other places
I can recall the size of an atom	☺ 😐 ☹	☺ 😐 ☹	☺ 😐 ☹		
I can recall the structure of an atom	☺ 😐 ☹	☺ 😐 ☹	☺ 😐 ☹	https://youtu.be/ljyzVt8bJSA	
I can recall the parts of an atom	☺ 😐 ☹	☺ 😐 ☹	☺ 😐 ☹		
I can recall the mass, charge and location of the subatomic particles	☺ 😐 ☹	☺ 😐 ☹	☺ 😐 ☹		
I can recall the electrons are arranged in energy levels (shells)	☺ 😐 ☹	☺ 😐 ☹	☺ 😐 ☹	https://youtu.be/bgWKesHbLnE	
I can explain that the position of electrons may change with the absorption or emission of electromagnetic radiation	☺ 😐 ☹	☺ 😐 ☹	☺ 😐 ☹		
I can define the terms atomic number and mass number	☺ 😐 ☹	☺ 😐 ☹	☺ 😐 ☹	https://youtu.be/ljyzVt8bJSA	
I can work out the number of protons, electrons and neutrons an atom has	☺ 😐 ☹	☺ 😐 ☹	☺ 😐 ☹	https://youtu.be/CEJ8WoNFFSI	
I can explain why atoms have no overall charge	☺ 😐 ☹	☺ 😐 ☹	☺ 😐 ☹	https://youtu.be/M5qfMT-ePrQ	
I can explain why ions have a charge	☺ 😐 ☹	☺ 😐 ☹	☺ 😐 ☹	https://youtu.be/746sTyJqrJo	
I can define the term isotope	☺ 😐 ☹	☺ 😐 ☹	☺ 😐 ☹	https://youtu.be/fIC2B935oXQ	
I can work out the number of protons, electrons and neutrons and isotope has	☺ 😐 ☹	☺ 😐 ☹	☺ 😐 ☹		
I can describe how and why a scientific model changes over time	☺ 😐 ☹	☺ 😐 ☹	☺ 😐 ☹		

I can describe the plum pudding model of the atom	☺ 😐 ☹	☺ 😐 ☹	☺ 😐 ☹	https://youtu.be/nbwcngWsXAU	
I can explain why Rutherford's experiment that disproved the plum pudding model	☺ 😐 ☹	☺ 😐 ☹	☺ 😐 ☹		
I can describe how Bohr adapted the model of the atom	☺ 😐 ☹	☺ 😐 ☹	☺ 😐 ☹		
I can recall what Chadwick added to the model of the atom	☺ 😐 ☹	☺ 😐 ☹	☺ 😐 ☹		
I can describe the process of radioactive decay	☺ 😐 ☹	☺ 😐 ☹	☺ 😐 ☹		
I can recall that activity is measured in Becquerel's (Bq)	☺ 😐 ☹	☺ 😐 ☹	☺ 😐 ☹		
I can describe what a Geiger-Muller tubes does	☺ 😐 ☹	☺ 😐 ☹	☺ 😐 ☹		
I can describe the different types of radiation	☺ 😐 ☹	☺ 😐 ☹	☺ 😐 ☹	https://youtu.be/NzGkp8ZcjZ0	
I can represent radioactive decay by nuclear equations	☺ 😐 ☹	☺ 😐 ☹	☺ 😐 ☹	https://youtu.be/L99xBAZY4AE	
I can define the term half-life	☺ 😐 ☹	☺ 😐 ☹	☺ 😐 ☹		
I can relate half-life to radioactive decay	☺ 😐 ☹	☺ 😐 ☹	☺ 😐 ☹	https://youtu.be/A9ej_7z03O8	
I can determine half-life from graphic or mathematical information	☺ 😐 ☹	☺ 😐 ☹	☺ 😐 ☹		
I can describe what radioactive contamination is	☺ 😐 ☹	☺ 😐 ☹	☺ 😐 ☹		
I can describe the precautions that need to be taken around radioactive contamination	☺ 😐 ☹	☺ 😐 ☹	☺ 😐 ☹		
I can recall the different sources of background radiation -**Physics only**	☺ 😐 ☹	☺ 😐 ☹	☺ 😐 ☹	https://youtu.be/LlVoVvpeQ5o	
I can describe what may affect a person dose of radiation -**Physics only**	☺ 😐 ☹	☺ 😐 ☹	☺ 😐 ☹		
I can recall that different isotopes have different half lives -**Physics only**	☺ 😐 ☹	☺ 😐 ☹	☺ 😐 ☹		
I can describe the different uses of radioactivity -**Physics only**	☺ 😐 ☹	☺ 😐 ☹	☺ 😐 ☹	https://youtu.be/LeRaJN2WpV0	

I can describe nuclear fission -Physics only	☺ 😐 ☹	☺ 😐 ☹	☺ 😐 ☹	https://youtu.be/uP0tWCLzorY	
I can describe the chain reaction that can occur from nuclear fission -Physics only	☺ 😐 ☹	☺ 😐 ☹	☺ 😐 ☹		
I can describe nuclear fusion -Physics only	☺ 😐 ☹	☺ 😐 ☹	☺ 😐 ☹	https://youtu.be/Iek-hpiMhTs	

Quick fire questions;

This worksheet is fully supported by a video tutorial; https://youtu.be/bRzRjfvoU-E

1. How big is an atom?
2. What is the mass of a proton?
3. What is the mass of a neutron?
4. What is the mass of an electron?
5. What is the charge on a proton?
6. What is the charge on an electron?
7. What is the charge on a neutron?
8. Where are protons found?
9. Where are neutrons found?
10. Where are electrons found?
11. What happens to electrons when they absorb or emit radiation?
12. What is the atomic number?
13. What is the mass number?
14. How do you find the number of protons an atom has?
15. How do you find the number of electrons an atom has?
16. How do you find the number of neutrons an atom has?
17. Why do atoms have no overall charge?
18. How do ions get charged?
19. What is an isotope?
20. What was the plum-pudding model?
21. What did Rutherford do?
22. What did Bohr do?
23. What did Chadwick do?
24. What is radioactive decay?
25. What are the units for radioactivity?
26. What are the three different types of radiation?
27. What is half-life?

Physics only

28. What the sources of background radiation?
29. What is nuclear fusion?
30. What is nuclear fission?

5 – Forces

Knowledge Checklist

Specification statement These are the bits the exam board wants you to know, make sure you can do all of these…	Self-assessment			Bits to help if you don't understand	
	First review 4-7 months before exam	Second review 1-2 months before exam	Final review Week before exam	Primrose Kitten	Other places
I can define the terms scalar and vector quantities	☺ 😐 ☹	☺ 😐 ☹	☺ 😐 ☹	https://youtu.be/ 5Xcie8V-UTw	
I can give examples of contact and non-contact forces	☺ 😐 ☹	☺ 😐 ☹	☺ 😐 ☹		
I can represent the forces acting on an object as vectors	☺ 😐 ☹	☺ 😐 ☹	☺ 😐 ☹		
I can calculate the resultant force on an object	☺ 😐 ☹	☺ 😐 ☹	☺ 😐 ☹	https://youtu.be/ Oa9LglsNm2o	
I can recall the difference between weight and mass	☺ 😐 ☹	☺ 😐 ☹	☺ 😐 ☹		
I can recall how to measure weight	☺ 😐 ☹	☺ 😐 ☹	☺ 😐 ☹		
I can recall the units needed for $W = mg$	☺ 😐 ☹	☺ 😐 ☹	☺ 😐 ☹		Flashcards available on www.primrose kitten.com
I can rearrange $W = mg$	☺ 😐 ☹	☺ 😐 ☹	☺ 😐 ☹		
I can use $W = mg$	☺ 😐 ☹	☺ 😐 ☹	☺ 😐 ☹		
I can describe what happens to an object when work is done on it	☺ 😐 ☹	☺ 😐 ☹	☺ 😐 ☹		
I can recall the units needed for $W = Fs$	☺ 😐 ☹	☺ 😐 ☹	☺ 😐 ☹		Flashcards available on www.primrose kitten.com
I can rearrange $W = Fs$	☺ 😐 ☹	☺ 😐 ☹	☺ 😐 ☹		
I can use $W = Fs$	☺ 😐 ☹	☺ 😐 ☹	☺ 😐 ☹		
I can convert between joules and newton-meters	☺ 😐 ☹	☺ 😐 ☹	☺ 😐 ☹		

I can explain why an object may change shape when a force is applied	☺ 😐 ☹	☺ 😐 ☹	☺ 😐 ☹		
I can explain what happens to an elastic object up to and then beyond the limit or proportionality	☺ 😐 ☹	☺ 😐 ☹	☺ 😐 ☹		
I can recall the units needed for F = ke	☺ 😐 ☹	☺ 😐 ☹	☺ 😐 ☹		Flashcards available on www.primrosekitten.com
I can rearrange F = ke	☺ 😐 ☹	☺ 😐 ☹	☺ 😐 ☹		
I can use F = ke	☺ 😐 ☹	☺ 😐 ☹	☺ 😐 ☹		
I can recall the units needed for $E_e = \frac{1}{2} ke^2$	☺ 😐 ☹	☺ 😐 ☹	☺ 😐 ☹		Flashcards available on www.primrosekitten.com
I can rearrange $E_e = \frac{1}{2} ke^2$	☺ 😐 ☹	☺ 😐 ☹	☺ 😐 ☹		
I can use $E_e = \frac{1}{2} ke^2$	☺ 😐 ☹	☺ 😐 ☹	☺ 😐 ☹		
I can describe how application of a force can cause an object to rotate -Physics only	☺ 😐 ☹	☺ 😐 ☹	☺ 😐 ☹	https://youtu.be/73t8QjZvMVI https://youtu.be/UiqGL-DCaBI https://youtu.be/WpT655stxUQ https://youtu.be/6aAljgK3kx8	
I can recall the units needed for M = Fd -Physics only	☺ 😐 ☹	☺ 😐 ☹	☺ 😐 ☹		Flashcards available on www.primrosekitten.com
I can rearrange M = Fd -Physics only	☺ 😐 ☹	☺ 😐 ☹	☺ 😐 ☹		
I can use M = Fd -Physics only	☺ 😐 ☹	☺ 😐 ☹	☺ 😐 ☹		
I can describe what happens to an object if the clockwise and anti-clockwise forces are balanced or unbalanced -Physics only	☺ 😐 ☹	☺ 😐 ☹	☺ 😐 ☹		
I can explain how levers and gears work -Physics only	☺ 😐 ☹	☺ 😐 ☹	☺ 😐 ☹		
I can recall that a fluid can be either liquid or a gas	☺ 😐 ☹	☺ 😐 ☹	☺ 😐 ☹		
I can state that liquids are incompressible	☺ 😐 ☹	☺ 😐 ☹	☺ 😐 ☹		

I can recall the units needed for $p = \dfrac{F}{A}$	☺ 😐 ☹	☺ 😐 ☹	☺ 😐 ☹		Flashcards available on www.primrose kitten.com
I can rearrange $p = \dfrac{F}{A}$	☺ 😐 ☹	☺ 😐 ☹	☺ 😐 ☹		
I can use $p = \dfrac{F}{A}$	☺ 😐 ☹	☺ 😐 ☹	☺ 😐 ☹		
I can calculate pressure at different points in a liquid **Higher Tier Only**	☺ 😐 ☹	☺ 😐 ☹	☺ 😐 ☹		
I can describe the factors which cause an object to either sink or float **Higher Tier Only**	☺ 😐 ☹	☺ 😐 ☹	☺ 😐 ☹		
I can recall the units needed for $p = h\rho g$ **Higher Tier Only**	☺ 😐 ☹	☺ 😐 ☹	☺ 😐 ☹		Flashcards available on www.primrose kitten.com
I can rearrange $p = h\rho g$ **Higher Tier Only**	☺ 😐 ☹	☺ 😐 ☹	☺ 😐 ☹		
I can use $p = h\rho g$ **Higher Tier Only**	☺ 😐 ☹	☺ 😐 ☹	☺ 😐 ☹		
I can describe how the atmosphere around the Earth changes as the distance from the Earth changes **Higher Tier Only**	☺ 😐 ☹	☺ 😐 ☹	☺ 😐 ☹		
I can describe distance as a scalar quantity	☺ 😐 ☹	☺ 😐 ☹	☺ 😐 ☹	https://youtu.be/ 5Xcie8V-UTw	
I can describe displacement as a vector quantity	☺ 😐 ☹	☺ 😐 ☹	☺ 😐 ☹		
I can describe speed as a scalar quantity	☺ 😐 ☹	☺ 😐 ☹	☺ 😐 ☹	https://youtu.be/ 5Xcie8V-UTw	
I can describe velocity as a vector quantity	☺ 😐 ☹	☺ 😐 ☹	☺ 😐 ☹	https://youtu.be/ Nfm0a1Ui5pw	
I can recall the units needed for $s = vt$	☺ 😐 ☹	☺ 😐 ☹	☺ 😐 ☹		Flashcards available on www.primrose kitten.com
I can rearrange $s = vt$	☺ 😐 ☹	☺ 😐 ☹	☺ 😐 ☹		
I can use $s = vt$	☺ 😐 ☹	☺ 😐 ☹	☺ 😐 ☹		

I can state that the speed of an object is constantly changing	☺ 😐 ☹	☺ 😐 ☹	☺ 😐 ☹		
I can draw and interpret distance-time graphs	☺ 😐 ☹	☺ 😐 ☹	☺ 😐 ☹	https://youtu.be/7OEL6bupk8A	
I can calculate the speed of an object from a distance time graph	☺ 😐 ☹	☺ 😐 ☹	☺ 😐 ☹		
I can describe the difference between speed and velocity	☺ 😐 ☹	☺ 😐 ☹	☺ 😐 ☹		
I can describe situations where an object has a constant speed but is accelerating	☺ 😐 ☹	☺ 😐 ☹	☺ 😐 ☹		
I can draw and interpret velocity-time graphs	☺ 😐 ☹	☺ 😐 ☹	☺ 😐 ☹	https://youtu.be/ZTwy8BYOhCs	
I can calculate the distance travelled by an object from a velocity-time graph	☺ 😐 ☹	☺ 😐 ☹	☺ 😐 ☹		
I can define acceleration	☺ 😐 ☹	☺ 😐 ☹	☺ 😐 ☹		
I can calculate the acceleration of an object from a velocity-time graph	☺ 😐 ☹	☺ 😐 ☹	☺ 😐 ☹	https://youtu.be/ZTwy8BYOhCs	
I can recall the units needed for $a = \frac{\Delta v}{t}$	☺ 😐 ☹	☺ 😐 ☹	☺ 😐 ☹		Flashcards available on www.primrosekitten.com
I can rearrange $a = \frac{\Delta v}{t}$	☺ 😐 ☹	☺ 😐 ☹	☺ 😐 ☹		
I can use $a = \frac{\Delta v}{t}$	☺ 😐 ☹	☺ 😐 ☹	☺ 😐 ☹		
I can recall the units needed for $v^2 - u^2 = 2as$	☺ 😐 ☹	☺ 😐 ☹	☺ 😐 ☹		Flashcards available on www.primrosekitten.com
I can rearrange $v^2 - u^2 = 2as$	☺ 😐 ☹	☺ 😐 ☹	☺ 😐 ☹		
I can use $v^2 - u^2 = 2as$	☺ 😐 ☹	☺ 😐 ☹	☺ 😐 ☹		
I can recall that an object free falling due to the force of gravity has an acceleration of $9.8 m/s^2$	☺ 😐 ☹	☺ 😐 ☹	☺ 😐 ☹		
I can describe how an object reaches terminal velocity	☺ 😐 ☹	☺ 😐 ☹	☺ 😐 ☹		

I can draw and interpret velocity-time graphs for objects that have reached terminal velocity	☺ 😐 ☹	☺ 😐 ☹	☺ 😐 ☹		
I can describe the forces on a moving object	☺ 😐 ☹	☺ 😐 ☹	☺ 😐 ☹		
I can describe how an object is moving if the resultant force on it is 0	☺ 😐 ☹	☺ 😐 ☹	☺ 😐 ☹	https://youtu.be/ Oa9LglsNm2o	
I can apply Newton's First Law to explain the motion of objects	☺ 😐 ☹	☺ 😐 ☹	☺ 😐 ☹		
I can describe inertia	☺ 😐 ☹	☺ 😐 ☹	☺ 😐 ☹		
I can describe the relationship between the mass of an object and its acceleration	☺ 😐 ☹	☺ 😐 ☹	☺ 😐 ☹		
I can recall the units needed for F = ma	☺ 😐 ☹	☺ 😐 ☹	☺ 😐 ☹		Flashcards available on www.primrose kitten.com
I can rearrange F = ma	☺ 😐 ☹	☺ 😐 ☹	☺ 😐 ☹		
I can use F = ma	☺ 😐 ☹	☺ 😐 ☹	☺ 😐 ☹		
I can describe what happens when two objects interact	☺ 😐 ☹	☺ 😐 ☹	☺ 😐 ☹		
I can describe stopping distance as a combination of reaction time and breaking distance	☺ 😐 ☹	☺ 😐 ☹	☺ 😐 ☹		
I can describe the factors that affect reaction time	☺ 😐 ☹	☺ 😐 ☹	☺ 😐 ☹		
I can describe the factors that affect breaking distance	☺ 😐 ☹	☺ 😐 ☹	☺ 😐 ☹		
I can explain features in a car that are design to make it safer	☺ 😐 ☹	☺ 😐 ☹	☺ 😐 ☹		
I can describe momentum as a property of moving objects **Higher Tier Only**	☺ 😐 ☹	☺ 😐 ☹	☺ 😐 ☹		
I can state the law of conservation of momentum **Higher Tier Only**	☺ 😐 ☹	☺ 😐 ☹	☺ 😐 ☹		
I can recall the units needed for p = mv **Higher Tier Only**	☺ 😐 ☹	☺ 😐 ☹	☺ 😐 ☹		Flashcards available on www.primrose kitten.com
I can rearrange p = mv **Higher Tier Only**	☺ 😐 ☹	☺ 😐 ☹	☺ 😐 ☹		

I can use p = mv **Higher Tier Only**	☺ ☻ ☹	☺ ☻ ☹	☺ ☻ ☹		
I can calculate momentum when two objects collide **Physics only**	☺ ☻ ☹	☺ ☻ ☹	☺ ☻ ☹		
I can recall the units needed for $F = \frac{m \Delta v}{\Delta t}$ **Physics only**	☺ ☻ ☹	☺ ☻ ☹	☺ ☻ ☹		Flashcards available on www.primrose kitten.com
I can rearrange $F = \frac{m \Delta v}{\Delta t}$ **Physics only**	☺ ☻ ☹	☺ ☻ ☹	☺ ☻ ☹		
I can use $F = \frac{m \Delta v}{\Delta t}$ **Physics only**	☺ ☻ ☹	☺ ☻ ☹	☺ ☻ ☹		

Quick Fire Questions

This worksheet is fully supported by a video tutorial; https://youtu.be/jfjb1pnH8zw

1. Define scaler quantity.
2. Define vector quantity.
3. Give an example of a contact force.
4. Given an example of a non-contact force.
5. How do you calculate resultant force?
6. What is the difference between mass and weight?
7. What is the equation linking weight, mass and gravity?
8. What are the units for weight?
9. What are the units for mass?
10. What are the units for gravity?
11. What is equation linking work, force and distance?
12. What are the units for work?
13. What are the units for force?
14. What are the units for distance?
15. How do you convert between Joules and Newton-metres?
16. What happens to an elastic object up to the limit of proportionality?
17. What happens to an elastic object after the limit of proportionality?
18. What is equation linking force, the spring constant and extension?
19. What are the units for force?
20. What the units for the spring constant?
21. What are the units for extension?
22. What is the equation linking elastic potential energy, the spring constant and extension?
23. What are the units for elastic potential energy?
24. What are the units for the spring constant?
25. What are the units for extension?
26. What is a fluid?
27. Can a fluid be compressed?
28. What is equation linking pressure, force and area?
29. What are the units for pressure?
30. What are the units for force?
31. What are the units for area?
32. Is distance a scalar or vector quantity?
33. Is displacement a scalar or vector quantity?
34. Is speed a scalar or vector quantity?
35. Is velocity a scalar or vector quantity?

36. What is the equation linking distance, velocity and time?
37. What are the units for distance?
38. What are the units for velocity?
39. What are the units for time?
40. How do you calculate the speed of an object from a distance-time graph?
41. When can an object have constant speed but still be accelerating?
42. How do you calculate the distance travelled from a velocity-time graph?
43. What is acceleration?
44. How do you calculate acceleration from a velocity-time graph?
45. What is the equation linking acceleration, change of in velocity and distance?
46. What are the units for acceleration?
47. What are the units for change in velocity?
48. What are the units of time?
49. What is the equation linking final velocity, initial velocity, acceleration and time?
50. If an object is falling due to gravity what acceleration does it have?
51. Define terminal velocity.
52. How is an object moving if the resultant force is zero?
53. What is Newton's first law.
54. Define inertia.
55. What is the equation linking force, mass and acceleration?
56. What are the units for force?
57. What are the units for mass?
58. What are the units for acceleration?
59. What is stopping distance?
60. Give two factors that can affect reaction time.
61. Give two factors that can affect braking distance.

Higher tier only

62. What factors can cause an object to float or sink?
63. What is equation linking pressure, height, density and gravitational field strength?
64. What are the units for pressure?
65. What are the units for height?
66. What are the units for density?
67. What are the units and value for gravitational field strength?
68. What is the law of conservation of the momentum?
69. What is equation linking the momentum, mass and velocity?
70. What are the units for momentum?
71. What are the units for mass?
72. What are the units for velocity?

Physics Only

73. What is equation linking moment, force and distance?
74. What are the units for moment?
75. What are the units for force?
76. What are the units the for distance?
77. What happens to an object if the clockwise and anticlockwise forces are balanced?
78. What happens to an object if the clockwise anticlockwise forces are unbalanced?
79. What is the equation linking force, mass, change in velocity and change the time?

6 – Waves

Knowledge Checklist

Specification statement These are the bits the exam board wants you to know, make sure you can do all of these…	Self-assessment			Bits to help if you don't understand	
	First review 4-7 months before exam	Second review 1-2 months before exam	Final review Week before exam	Primrose Kitten	Other places
I can draw and label transverse and longitudinal waves	☺ 😐 ☹	☺ 😐 ☹	☺ 😐 ☹		
I can describe the direction of movement and the direction of energy transfer for both transverse and longitudinal waves	☺ 😐 ☹	☺ 😐 ☹	☺ 😐 ☹		
I can define the terms, amplitude, wavelength and frequency	☺ 😐 ☹	☺ 😐 ☹	☺ 😐 ☹		
I can recall the units needed for $T = \frac{1}{f}$	☺ 😐 ☹	☺ 😐 ☹	☺ 😐 ☹		Flashcards available on www.primrosekitten.com
I can rearrange $T = \frac{1}{f}$	☺ 😐 ☹	☺ 😐 ☹	☺ 😐 ☹		
I can use $T = \frac{1}{F}$	☺ 😐 ☹	☺ 😐 ☹	☺ 😐 ☹		
I can describe how to measure the speed of waves	☺ 😐 ☹	☺ 😐 ☹	☺ 😐 ☹		
I can recall the units needed for $v = f\lambda$	☺ 😐 ☹	☺ 😐 ☹	☺ 😐 ☹		Flashcards available on www.primrosekitten.com
I can rearrange $v = f\lambda$	☺ 😐 ☹	☺ 😐 ☹	☺ 😐 ☹		
I can use $v = f\lambda$	☺ 😐 ☹	☺ 😐 ☹	☺ 😐 ☹		

I can construct ray diagrams to show what happens to a wave when it is reflected **Physics only**	☺ 😐 ☹	☺ 😐 ☹	☺ 😐 ☹		
I can describe what happens to a wave when it hits a boundary **Physics only**	☺ 😐 ☹	☺ 😐 ☹	☺ 😐 ☹		
I can describe how a sound wave travels **Higher tier only** **Physics only**	☺ 😐 ☹	☺ 😐 ☹	☺ 😐 ☹		
I can describe how an ear detects sound **Higher tier only** **Physics only**	☺ 😐 ☹	☺ 😐 ☹	☺ 😐 ☹		
I can recall the range of human hearing **Higher tier only** **Physics only**	☺ 😐 ☹	☺ 😐 ☹	☺ 😐 ☹		
I can explain how echo can be used to determine distances **Higher tier only** **Physics only**	☺ 😐 ☹	☺ 😐 ☹	☺ 😐 ☹		
I can explain how changes in a wave can be used for detection and exploration **Higher tier only** **Physics only**	☺ 😐 ☹	☺ 😐 ☹	☺ 😐 ☹		
I can describe what happens to an ultrasound wave when it hits a boundary and how this property can be used for imaging **Higher tier only** **Physics only**	☺ 😐 ☹	☺ 😐 ☹	☺ 😐 ☹		
I can describe how information from P-waves and S-waves can be used to provide evidence for the structure of the Earth **Higher tier only** **Physics only**	☺ 😐 ☹	☺ 😐 ☹	☺ 😐 ☹		

I can recall the order of the electromagnetic waves	☺ 😐 ☹	☺ 😐 ☹	☺ 😐 ☹		
I can recall that electromagnetic waves are transverse and form a continue spectrum	☺ 😐 ☹	☺ 😐 ☹	☺ 😐 ☹		
I can recall uses and properties of each part of the spectrum	☺ 😐 ☹	☺ 😐 ☹	☺ 😐 ☹		
I can draw a ray diagram to show what happens when a wave is diffracted **Higher tier only**	☺ 😐 ☹	☺ 😐 ☹	☺ 😐 ☹		
I can describe what happens to the path of a wave when is refracted **Higher tier only**	☺ 😐 ☹	☺ 😐 ☹	☺ 😐 ☹		
I can explain why refraction happen **Higher tier only**	☺ 😐 ☹	☺ 😐 ☹	☺ 😐 ☹	https://youtu.be/CrC1IlSy-bQ	
I can explain how an alternating current may produce radio waves **Higher tier only**	☺ 😐 ☹	☺ 😐 ☹	☺ 😐 ☹		
I can describe that a wave may be absorb, transmitted, refracted or reflected when it hits a surface **Higher tier only**	☺ 😐 ☹	☺ 😐 ☹	☺ 😐 ☹		
I can recall which surfaces absorb, emit and radiation **Higher tier only**	☺ 😐 ☹	☺ 😐 ☹	☺ 😐 ☹		
I can describe the circumstances in which a converging lens should be used **Physics only**	☺ 😐 ☹	☺ 😐 ☹	☺ 😐 ☹	https://youtu.be/4H9PAx90qMQ https://youtu.be/19SLrBwZYSA https://youtu.be/aRDt8PUhv4c	
I can construct a ray diagram for a converging lens **Physics only**	☺ 😐 ☹	☺ 😐 ☹	☺ 😐 ☹		
I can describe the image formed by a converging lens **Physics only**	☺ 😐 ☹	☺ 😐 ☹	☺ 😐 ☹		

I can describe the circumstances in which a diverging lens should be used **Physics only**	☺ 😐 ☹	☺ 😐 ☹	☺ 😐 ☹		
I can construct a ray diagram for a diverging lens **Physics only**	☺ 😐 ☹	☺ 😐 ☹	☺ 😐 ☹		
I can describe the image formed by a diverging lens **Physics only**	☺ 😐 ☹	☺ 😐 ☹	☺ 😐 ☹		
I can rearrange Magnification = image height / object height **Physics only**	☺ 😐 ☹	☺ 😐 ☹	☺ 😐 ☹	https://youtu.be/v-KrUP3bu24	
I can use Magnification = image height / object height **Physics only**	☺ 😐 ☹	☺ 😐 ☹	☺ 😐 ☹		
I can recall the order of light in the visible spectrum **Physics only**	☺ 😐 ☹	☺ 😐 ☹	☺ 😐 ☹		
I can recall the relative wavelengths and frequencies of the different parts of the visible light spectrum **Physics only**	☺ 😐 ☹	☺ 😐 ☹	☺ 😐 ☹		
I can describe that objects absorb and transmit light of different wavelengths **Physics only**	☺ 😐 ☹	☺ 😐 ☹	☺ 😐 ☹		
I can describe the difference between objects that are opaque, transparent and translucent **Physics only**	☺ 😐 ☹	☺ 😐 ☹	☺ 😐 ☹		
I can describe what happen to light when it is passed through a filter **Physics only**	☺ 😐 ☹	☺ 😐 ☹	☺ 😐 ☹		
I can recall that all objects emit infrared radiation **Physics only**	☺ 😐 ☹	☺ 😐 ☹	☺ 😐 ☹		

I can explain what a perfect black body is **Physics only**	☺ 😐 ☹	☺ 😐 ☹	☺ 😐 ☹		
I can explain that the intensity and wavelength distribution depends on the temperature of the object **Physics only**	☺ 😐 ☹	☺ 😐 ☹	☺ 😐 ☹		
I can explain anybody is constantly absorbing and emitting radiation, and the balanced between the two determines the temperature **Physics only**	☺ 😐 ☹	☺ 😐 ☹	☺ 😐 ☹		

Quick Fire Questions

This worksheet is fully supported by a video tutorial; https://youtu.be/AEFwEDC6DkQ

1. Sketch and label a transverse wave.
2. Sketch and label a longitudinal wave.
3. Define amplitude.
4. Define wavelength.
5. What is equation linking time period and frequency?
6. What are the units for time period?
7. What are the units for frequency?
8. What is equation linking wave speed, frequency and wavelength?
9. What are the units for wavelength?
10. What are the units for wave speed?
11. What is order of the electromagnetic waves?
12. What can radio-waves be used for?
13. What can microwaves be used for
14. What can infrared be used for?
15. What can visible light be used for?
16. What can ultraviolet be used for?
17. What can gamma rays be used for?
18. What can x-rays be used for?

Higher tier only

19. What happens when a wave is diffracted?
20. What happens when a wave is refracted?
21. Why does refraction happen?
22. Which surfaces absorb radiation?
23. Which surfaces emit radiation?

Physics only

24. What image is formed by converging lens?
25. When can converging lens be used?
26. When should a diverging lens be used?
27. What image is formed by diverging lens?
28. How do you calculate magnification?
29. What are the units for magnification?
30. What is the order of light in the visible spectrum?

31. What does opaque mean?
32. What does transparent mean?
33. What does translucent mean?
34. What happens to light when is passes through a filter?

Higher tier only

35. How to soundwaves travel?
36. What is the range of human hearing?
37. What is the P-wave?
38. What is an S-wave?

7 - Magnetism and Electromagnets

Knowledge Checklist

Specification statement These are the bits the exam board wants you to know, make sure you can do all of these...	Self-assessment			Bits to help if you don't understand	
	First review 4-7 months before exam	Second review 1-2 months before exam	Final review Week before exam	Primrose Kitten	Other places
I can describe what happens when two like or unlike poles are placed next to each other	☺ 😐 ☹	☺ 😐 ☹	☺ 😐 ☹		
I can describe that a permanent magnet also has a magnetic field	☺ 😐 ☹	☺ 😐 ☹	☺ 😐 ☹		
I can recall that an induced magnet is a temporary magnet, when placed in a magnetic field	☺ 😐 ☹	☺ 😐 ☹	☺ 😐 ☹		
I can recall which materials are magnetic	☺ 😐 ☹	☺ 😐 ☹	☺ 😐 ☹		
I can relate the strength of the magnetic field to the proximity of the object	☺ 😐 ☹	☺ 😐 ☹	☺ 😐 ☹		
I can describe the direction of a magnetic field	☺ 😐 ☹	☺ 😐 ☹	☺ 😐 ☹	https://youtu.be/V0OkOHKIcjQ	
I can plot a magnetic field	☺ 😐 ☹	☺ 😐 ☹	☺ 😐 ☹		
I can describe how a current can produce a magnetic field	☺ 😐 ☹	☺ 😐 ☹	☺ 😐 ☹		
I can describe how to change the strength of an electromagnet	☺ 😐 ☹	☺ 😐 ☹	☺ 😐 ☹		
I can explain how an electromagnet works	☺ 😐 ☹	☺ 😐 ☹	☺ 😐 ☹	https://youtu.be/OBvFwTaIca8 https://youtu.be/6GMAK_evAz8	
I can use Flemings left hand rule to find the direction of the force **Higher tier only**	☺ 😐 ☹	☺ 😐 ☹	☺ 😐 ☹	https://youtu.be/whfpEeoHxNw	

I can recall what factors affect the size of the force **Higher tier only**	☺ ☺ ☹	☺ ☺ ☹	☺ ☺ ☹		
I can define magnetic flux density **Higher tier only**	☺ ☺ ☹	☺ ☺ ☹	☺ ☺ ☹		
I can recall the units needed for $F = BIl$ **Higher tier only**	☺ ☺ ☹	☺ ☺ ☹	☺ ☺ ☹		Flashcards available on www.primrosekitten.com
I can rearrange $F = BIl$ **Higher tier only**	☺ ☺ ☹	☺ ☺ ☹	☺ ☺ ☹		
I can use $F = BIl$ **Higher tier only**	☺ ☺ ☹	☺ ☺ ☹	☺ ☺ ☹		
I can describe how an electric motor works **Higher tier only**	☺ ☺ ☹	☺ ☺ ☹	☺ ☺ ☹		
I can explain how the forces causes the rotation of the coil **Higher tier only**	☺ ☺ ☹	☺ ☺ ☹	☺ ☺ ☹		
I can explain how a moving-coil loudspeaker works **Higher tier only**	☺ ☺ ☹	☺ ☺ ☹	☺ ☺ ☹		
I can explain how a moving-coil microphone works **Higher tier only**	☺ ☺ ☹	☺ ☺ ☹	☺ ☺ ☹		
I can explain the generator effect **Higher tier only** **Physics only**	☺ ☺ ☹	☺ ☺ ☹	☺ ☺ ☹		
I can recall the factors that can affect the size of the induced potential **Higher tier only** **Physics only**	☺ ☺ ☹	☺ ☺ ☹	☺ ☺ ☹		
I can apply the generator effect **Higher tier only** **Physics only**	☺ ☺ ☹	☺ ☺ ☹	☺ ☺ ☹		
I can describe how the generator effect can produce ac and dc current **Higher tier only** **Physics only**	☺ ☺ ☹	☺ ☺ ☹	☺ ☺ ☹		

I can describe the structure of a transformer **Higher tier only** **Physics only**	☺ 😐 ☹	☺ 😐 ☹	☺ 😐 ☹	https://youtu.be/jXC2BvL-Ffk	
I can recall the units needed for $\frac{V_p}{V_s} = \frac{n_p}{n_s}$ **Higher tier only** **Physics only**	☺ 😐 ☹	☺ 😐 ☹	☺ 😐 ☹		Flashcards available on www.primrosekitten.com
I can rearrange $\frac{V_p}{V_s} = \frac{n_p}{n_s}$ **Higher tier only** **Physics only**	☺ 😐 ☹	☺ 😐 ☹	☺ 😐 ☹		
I can use $\frac{V_p}{V_s} = \frac{n_p}{n_s}$ **Higher tier only** **Physics only**	☺ 😐 ☹	☺ 😐 ☹	☺ 😐 ☹		
I can recall the units needed for $V_s I_s = V_p I_p$ **Higher tier only** **Physics only**	☺ 😐 ☹	☺ 😐 ☹	☺ 😐 ☹		Flashcards available on www.primrosekitten.com
I can rearrange $V_s I_s = V_p I_p$ **Higher tier only** **Physics only**	☺ 😐 ☹	☺ 😐 ☹	☺ 😐 ☹		
I can use $V_s I_s = V_p I_p$ **Higher tier only** **Physics only**	☺ 😐 ☹	☺ 😐 ☹	☺ 😐 ☹		

Quick Fire Questions

This worksheet is fully supported by a video tutorial; https://youtu.be/LyflUYL4FvM

1. What happens when you place like poles on a magnet next to each other?
2. What happens when you place unlike poles on a magnet next to each other?
3. Which materials are magnetic?
4. What is the direction of the magnetic field?
5. How do you change strength of an electromagnet?

Higher Tier Only

6. Define magnetic flux density.
7. What is the equation linking force, magnetic flux density, current and length?
8. What are the units for force?
9. What are the units for magnetic flux density?
10. What are the units for current?
11. What are the units for length?

Physics only

12. What is equation linking voltage at the primary coil, number of turns on the primary coil, voltage at the secondary coil, and number of turns on the secondary coil?
13. What are the units for voltage at the primary coil and voltage at the secondary coil?
14. What is equation linking voltage at the secondary coil, current at the secondary coil, voltage the primary coil, current at the primary coil?

8 - Space Physics - Physics only

Knowledge Checklist

Whole topic summary video; https://youtu.be/MdiOi24tNT0 in only 8 minutes!

| Specification statement

These are the bits the exam board wants you to know, make sure you can do all of these...	Self-assessment			Bits to help if you don't understand	
	First review 4-7 months before exam	Second review 1-2 months before exam	Final review Week before exam	Primrose Kitten	Other places
I can describe our Solar system	☺ ☻ ☹	☺ ☻ ☹	☺ ☻ ☹		
I can describe our galaxy	☺ ☻ ☹	☺ ☻ ☹	☺ ☻ ☹		
I can describe the life cycle of a star	☺ ☻ ☹	☺ ☻ ☹	☺ ☻ ☹	https://youtu.be/ STdwZe2GfEsv	
I can describe the processes that go on in the centre of a star	☺ ☻ ☹	☺ ☻ ☹	☺ ☻ ☹		
I can recall the difference between natural and artificial satellites	☺ ☻ ☹	☺ ☻ ☹	☺ ☻ ☹		
I can describe how an object maintains its orbit	☺ ☻ ☹	☺ ☻ ☹	☺ ☻ ☹		
I can describe how velocity can change while speed remains constant	☺ ☻ ☹	☺ ☻ ☹	☺ ☻ ☹		
I can describe how red and blue shift occur	☺ ☻ ☹	☺ ☻ ☹	☺ ☻ ☹		
I can explain what red and blue shift show use	☺ ☻ ☹	☺ ☻ ☹	☺ ☻ ☹		
I can explain how red shift provides evidence for the Big Bang	☺ ☻ ☹	☺ ☻ ☹	☺ ☻ ☹	https://youtu.be/ OlERzqXHXFw	

Quick Fire Questions

This worksheet is fully supported by a video tutorial; https://youtu.be/f3Rf1aVStIk

1. Give the order of objects in our solar system.
2. What is a galaxy?
3. Give the life cycle of a small star.
4. Give the life cycle of a large star.
5. What happens at the centre of a star?
6. What is a natural satellite?
7. What is an artificial satellite?
8. How does an object maintain its orbit?
9. How can an object change velocity while speed remains constant?
10. What is Redshift?
11. What is blue shift?
12. How does Redshift via evidence for the big bang?

Crosswords

Physics Units

Across

7) the units for force

9) the units for charge

10) the units for mass

11) the units for current

12) the units for time period

13) the units for power

14) the units for frequency

16) the units for pressure

18) the units for initial velocity

20) the units for volume

21) the units for specific latent heat

22) the units for density

Down

1) the units for the spring constant

2) the units for potential difference

3) the units for acceleration

4) the units for work done

5) the units for gravitational field strength

6) the units for moment

8) the units for area

15) the units for resistance

17) the units for length

19) the units for magnetic flux density

Answers

Biology crossword 1

Across

3) lump of cells that are not invading the body [BENIGNTUMOR]

5) carries oxygen around the body, has no nucleus [REDBLOODCELL]

7) small fragments of blood cells that help clotting [PLATELETS]

9) Thinned walled blood vessels that allow diffusion of gases and nutrients [CAPILLARY]

14) Enzyme that breaks carbohydrates into sugars [AMYLASE]

18) Small structural unit that contains a nucleus and cytoplasm [CELL]

19) fluid part of the blood [PLASMA]

20) one copy of each chromosome [HAPLOID]

23) organ system that absorbs nutrients from food [DIGESTIVESYSTEM]

26) Major blood vessel that carries deoxygenated blood back to the heart [VENACAVA]

28) state of mental and physical wellbeing [HEALTH]

29) Type of cell division that ends in two identical daughter cells [MITOSIS]

30) uncontrolled cell division within the body [CANCER]

31) Blood vessel that carries deoxygenated blood from the heart to the lungs [PULMONARYARTERY]

Down

1) Major blood vessel that carries oxygenated blood away from the heart [AORTA]

2) carries water around a plant [XYLEM]

4) organ system that moves oxygen around the body [RESPIRATORYSYSTEM]

6) Produced by the liver, neutralizes stomach acid and emulsifies fats [BILE]

8) the study of organism within and environment [ECOLOGY]

10) long stretch of DNA [CHROMOSOME]

11) Enzyme that breaks proteins into amino acids [PROTEASE]

12) jelly like substance within a cell [CYTOPLASM]

13) a type of cell that can differentiate into any other type of cell [STEMCELL]

15) two copies of each chromosome [DIPLOID]

16) control centre of the cell, that holds the DNA [NUCLEUS]

17) Biological catalyst [ENZYME]

21) movement of ions or gasses from a high concentration to a low concentration [DIFFUSION]

22) Enzyme that breaks fats into fatty acids and glycerol [LIPASE]

24) plant tissue found at growing tips [MERISTEM]

25) carries ions around a plant [PHLOEM]

27) Blood vessels that have values and carries deoxygenated blood back to the heart [VEIN]

Biology Crossword 2

Across

5) medication that contain inactive or dead virus to help develop immunity [VACCINES]

8) large gland in the neck which releases hormone [THYROID]

10) braches of the trachea [BRONCHI]

11) in women, these stores the eggs [OVARIES]

13) can be combined with glycerol to make lipids [FATTYACIDS]

14) DNA within a protein coat that divides by invading cells, the resulting cell death causes illness in the host [VIRUS]

17) parasite transmitted by mosquitoes [MALARIA]

21) system that controls hormones and responses [ENDOCRINESYSTEM]

23) inability of the bod to control blood glucose levels [DIABETES]

24) long chains of amino acids, that carry out the majority of functions within the body [PROTEINS]

27) drugs that kill bacteria [ANTIBIOTICS]

28) green part of a plant [CHLOROPHYLL]

29) in men, these are responsible for the production of sperm [TESTIS]

30) chemical process that occur to maintain life [METABOLISM]

31) arises after anaerobic respiration, needs oxygen to repay [OXYGENDEBT]

32) viral infection causing fever and rash, most common in children [MEASLES]

Down

1) causes illness [PATHOGEN]

2) large gland behind the stomach which produces digestive enzymes [PANCREAS]

3) respiration with oxygen [AEROBIC]

4) bacteria that cause a sexual transmitted disease causing smelly discharge from the penis or vagina [GONORRHEA]

6) stores of energy that can be broken down to form fatty acids and glycerol [LIPIDS]

7) long tube taking air down into the lungs [TRACHEA]

9) virus that interfere with your body's ability to fight disease [HIV]

12) painkiller developed from willow bark [ASPIRIN]

13) group that includes mushrooms and moulds, they live of decomposing material [FUNGI]

15) can be combined with fatty acid to make lipids [GLYCEROL]

16) process where plant absorb and lose water [TRANSPIRATION]

18) nerve pathway including a sensory nerve a synapse and a motor nerve [REFLEXARC]

19) large gland near the kidneys that releases hormone [ADRENALGLAND]

20) virus affecting plants causing a mosaic pattern on leaves [TMV]

22) tiny single celled organism that can cause illness [PROTIST]

25) heart drug that comes from Foxglove plants [DIGITALIS]

26) transport of water across a partially permeable membrane [OSMOSIS]

Biology crossword 3

Across

1) breading of animals or plants for a particular characteristic [SELECTIVEBREADING]

5) change in a spices to suit the environment [ADAPTATION]

9) sex cells [GAMETES]

10) different copies of gene [HETEROZYGOUS]

11) no breading pair of a species exist [EXTINCTION]

13) male sex cell [SPERM]

14) what genes are present [GENOTYPE]

17) eat plants and animals [OMNIVORE]

18) different version of gene [ALLELE]

22) two identical copies of the gene are needed to be expressed [RECESSIVE]

23) the range of different organism that live in an environment [BIODIVERSITY]

24) only one copy of the gene is needed to be expressed [DOMINANT]

25) section of DNA, that controls a characteristic [GENE]

Down

2) non-living factors that affect organism [ABIOTIC]

3) the movement of carbon through the environment [CARBONCYCLE]

4) mechanism to prevent pregnancy [CONTRACEPTION]

5) reproduction with only one parent, resulting in identical offspring [ASEXUALREPRODUCTION]

6) hormone found predominantly in men [TESTOSTERONE]

7) female sex cell [EGG]

8) identical copies of gene [HOMOZYGOUS]

11) the organism and the habitat they live in [ECOSYSTEM]

12) the organism that live in a particular environment [COMMUNITY]

15) harmful substance in an environment [POLLUTION]

16) the movement of water through eh environment [WATERCYCLE]

19) hard parts of long dead organism [FOSSILS]

20) all of the genes in an organism [GENOME]

21) something that gets eaten [PREY]

Chemistry Crossword 1

Across

6) a way of sorting out the elements [PERIODICTABLE]

10) group of (or single) atoms that all have the same chemical characteristics, can be found on the periodic table [ELEMENT]

12) group of metal that are in the middle of the periodic table, form colour compounds and can be used as catalysts [TRANSITIONMETAL]

14) found in the nucleus of atoms, has no charge and a mass of one [NEUTRON]

16) small part of matter, made up from a mixture of protons, neutrons and electrons [ATOM]

17) the number of protons and neutrons in an atom [MASSNUMBER]

21) transfer of electrons between a metal and a non-metal [IONICBONDING]

22) atoms that has lost or gained electrons [ION]

23) giant covalent compound where each carbons atom makes three bonds [GRAPHITE]

26) a way of determining how many of the reactant atoms made it into the desired product [ATOMECONOMY]

27) a state of matter, where the atoms can move and flow but they cannot be compressed [LIQUID]

28) the number of protons in an atom [ATOMICNUMBER]

29) a state of matter where the atoms move atom in a fast and random matter, can be compressed and flow [GAS]

Down

1) in the centre of atoms, contains the protons and the neutrons [NUCLEUS]

2) on the left-hand side of the periodic table, form positive ions [METAL]

3) method for determining concentration of solution [TITRATION]

4) highly reactive metals found on the left-hand side of the periodic table [ALKALIMETAL]

5) found in the shells around the nucleus, has a charge of minus one and no mass [ELECTRON]

7) a type of reaction where one element replaces another in a compound [DISPLACEMENT]

8) found in the nucleus of atoms, has a charge of plus one and a mass of one [PROTON]

9) sharing of electron between two non-metals [COVALENTBONDING]

11) on the right-hand side of the periodic table, form negative ions [NONMETAL]

13) lots of different elements that may or may not be chemically bonded together [MIXTURE]

15) giant covalent compound where each carbons atom makes four bonds [DIAMOND]

18) two or more elements chemically bonded together [COMPOUND]

19) unreactive gases found on the right of the periodic table [NOBELGAS]

20) mixture of atoms that lead to distorted layers that cannot slide [ALLOY]

24) a state of matter, where the atoms vibrate around a fixed position [SOLID]

25) the molecular mass in grams [MOLE]

Chemistry crossword 2

Across

1) burning of a compound in oxygen [COMBUSTION]

2) gain of electrons [REDUCTION]

5) breaking a long hydrocarbon chain to short hydrocarbon chains [CRACKING]

7) water that is safe to drink [PORTABLEWATER]

14) hydrocarbon containing double bonds [ALKENES]

15) point at which a solid turn into a liquid [MELTINGPOINT]

16) orange liquid that can be used to test for double bonds [BROMINEWATER]

18) mixing of an acid and an alkali to give a pH of 7 [NEUTRALIZATION]

20) how acid or alkali a solution is [PH]

21) loss of electrons [OXIDATION]

22) something that speeds up a react of reaction without being use dup [CATALYST]

23) how easily pourable something is [VISCOSITY]

Down

1) a mixture of different length hydrocarbon chains made from decomposing dead plant and animals [CRUDEOIL]

3) a reaction that releases energy [EXOTHERMIC]

4) a reaction that takes in energy [ENDOTHERMIC]

6) hydrocarbon containing only single bonds [ALKANES]

8) separating compounds using electricity [ELECTROLYSIS]

9) the energy needed to start reaction [ACTIVATIONENERGY]

10) gas that traps infra-red radiation [GREENHOUSEGAS]

11) a compound that only has carbon and hydrogen in it [HYDROCARBON]

12) method of separating out mixtures [CHROMATOGRAPHY]

13) mining low yield ores using plants [PHYTOMINING]

17) a solution that has a low pH due to the hydrogen ions [ACID]

19) a solution that has a high pH due to hydroxide ions [ALKALI]

Physics units

Across

7) the units for force [NEWTONS]

9) the units for charge [COULOMBS]

10) the units for mass [KILOGRAMS]

11) the units for current [AMPS]

12) the units for time period [SECONDS]

13) the units for power [WATT]

14) the units for frequency [HERTZ]

16) the units for pressure [PASCALS]

18) the units for initial velocity [METERSPERSECOND]

20) the units for volume [METERSCUBED]

21) the units for specific latent heat [JOULESPERKILOGRAM]

22) the units for density [KILOGRAMSPERMETERCUBED]

Down

1) the units for the spring constant [NEWTONSPERMETER]

2) the units for potential difference [VOLTS]

3) the units for acceleration [METERSPERSECONDSQUARED]

4) the units for work done [JOULES]

5) the units for gravitational field strength [NEWTONSPERKILOGRAM]

6) the units for moment [NEWTONMETERS]

8) the units for area [METERSSQUARED]

15) the units for resistance [OHMS]

17) the units for length [METERS]

19) the units for magnetic flux density [TESLA]

Printed in Poland
by Amazon Fulfillment
Poland Sp. z o.o., Wrocław